Oscar Emery Young

Seaside Songs and Woodland Whispers

Oscar Emery Young

Seaside Songs and Woodland Whispers

ISBN/EAN: 9783744649377

Printed in Europe, USA, Canada, Australia, Japan

Cover: Foto ©Thomas Meinert / pixelio.de

More available books at **www.hansebooks.com**

SEASIDE SONGS

AND

WOODLAND WHISPERS

BY

OSCAR E. YOUNG.

.

" Whoever thinks a faultless piece to see,
Thinks what ne'er was, nor is, nor e'er shalt be."

———

AUTHOR'S EDITION

———

BUFFALO
CHARLES WELLS MOULTON
1891

CONTENTS.

SEASIDE SONGS.

WOODLAND WHISPERS.

623936

Contents.   V

MISCELLANEOUS POEMS.

SEASIDE SONGS.

SEASIDE SONGS.

There's a voice comes up from the sounding sea
  With its pulsing bosom that throbs and swells.
As I sit and listen, it sings to me
A wild and a wonderful harmony,
  And I half interpret the tale it tells.

Down under the ocean's heaving breast
  The heart of Nature beats evermore,
And the thoughts there throbbing are half expressed
In the song it sings in its long unrest,
  As the waves sonorous roll on the shore.

In glittering sunlight, serenely fair,
  As the shining ripples caress the beach,
It sings of love and its raptures rare,
And murmurs a melody soft as prayer,
  A melody sweeter by far than speech.

When the stars look down through the shades of night
  With pitying eyes on the scene below,
Where their calm reflections are wavering bright,
Then the seaside song through the dusky light
  Thrills with tender sorrow and wordless woe.

But the howling storm-wind in tempest might
    Bears a battle hymn on the ocean's breath,
And it chants of crimes and of deeds of night,
Of the nameless horrors ne'er brought to light,
    Of mortal danger, despair and death.

The songs of the seaside reveal to me
    Strange, awful things in their mystic speech;
. Quaint tales, wild stories of mystery,
Fresh fancies, gleams of sublimity —
    All these, and more, to my soul they teach.

I have taken a point of the shining steel
    And dipped it deep in a dye of night,
And the wordless music, whose sense I feel,
That the ocean chants with its sounding peal,
    As my soul interprets it, so I write.

Long Island, Me., Nov. 20th, 1889.

A SEA DRÈAM.

Methought I floated on a starlit sea,
In the calm beauty of the summer moon
That shone in silver o'er me.   Like a cloud
Floating at even through the azure sky,
My light skiff floated on the dimpling deep
That rippled in the moonbeams, sending forth
A thousand thousand phosphorescent gleams
From its dark bosom.   In the vast above
The pale stars throbbed and trembled, while below
Their faint reflections swam and throbbed again.

From the dim distance, where the tree-clad shore
Showed indistinct in silver glory poured
From Luna's full-orbed shield, that hung above
And shed a mellow radiance on the scene,
Came the faint murmur of the rippling tide
Kissing the sandy beaches.   Hushed the winds
And tranquilized the waves ; and o'er the sea,
In the calm beauty of that perfect night,
Like a soul floating in unending rest,
In my frail bark I floated on alone.

But suddenly, methought, up from the deep
Came a soft strain of sweetest melody,
Like nothing earthly ever heard before.
Faint, strange and thrilling, blending with the chime .
Of the low murmur from the far-off shore,
And the calm, mystic beauty of the night,
Came the soft notes of perfect harmony,
Like half-heard echoes of an angel's song.

Through my rapt spirit crept the strain divine
With strange, bewitching power, and every nerve
Was throbbing, trembling with an ecstasy
As if my soul, intoxicated deep,
Had fed to fullness on the food of gods,
Or fire and honey blended.   And, as came
The music nearer, clearer than at first,
The wild, strange madness in my spirit grew,
Absorbing reason, almost thought itself.

Then suddenly before the pointed prow
The gleaming waves divided, rolling back
In drops of glittering silver from a form
That cleft their dim; cool bosoms.   From the deep
A shape of strange, unearthly beauty rose,
A sea-maid pale, with wildly streaming hair,
Like threads of amber from the deep sea caves,
Hiding the water where she rose and dipped
With the slow motion of voluptuous swells:

Breast-deep she floated in the pulsing sea,
Clad only in the glory of her hair,
That half revealed a form whose perfectness .
No sculptor ever dreamed of, and so white
That marble by its side would seem unclean,
And snow new-fallen as a thing defiled.

Oh, the smooth whiteness of the fair, pure throat,
The perfect, lucent features, rounded, soft,
Clear as if from some heavenly crystal cut,
And far surpassing all things earth e'er knew,
As pearl dark coal surpasses! And her eyes,
Large, tender, luminous, of wondrous tint
That mere words fail to picture! Somewhat like
The glorious gleaming of great emeralds,
Lying in watery radiance on the floor
Of some deep ocean bower, and somewhat like
The light that through the clear green water streams
Into the palaces of ocean-gods!

Out from the golden glimmer of her hair
And the dim darkness of the shadowy sea
Rose two fair arms of pure, unearthly white,
More perfect than an artist's dream of those
Of the pure Virgin Mother. In her hands
A wondrous shell of carven pearl she bore,
Studded with gleaming gems and strung with gold,
Which, as her perfect fingers o'er it strayed,
Gave forth the soft, sweet, throbbing melody

That held my spirit captive ; and her eyes,
Those wondrous, luminous, alluring eyes,
In which a wild, unearthly rapture gleamed,
From out the cloud of glory where she swam,
(For all the brightness of the moon and stars
Seemed gathered round her in a silver mist,)
Beamed into mine and filled my soul with fire.

Trembling and thrilling with the madness strange,
By all the sea-maid's wondrous charms enthralled,
Upon the rocking prow methought I sprang,
And cast upon that form and face divine,
Like carven ivory ten times purified,
A single glance ; then, in wild ecstasy,
I leaped into the siren's cold embrace
And felt the dead, white arms around me close.

Down, down into the dark, cold waves we sank,
The icy arms close clinging round my neck
And dragging me into the lowest depths,
Like tons of solid lead !   A roaring noise,
Like that of countless mighty deluges,
Throbbed in my ears and beat upon my brain ;
Countless electric flashes seared my eyes
With fiery sparkles of tormenting pain,
And all my form was racked with agony.

I felt my prisoned spirit in me swell,
And beat, and struggle to burst through the bars
That shut it in my body.   Like the throes

Within some vast volcano's fiery heart,
When the imprisoned lava rolls and heaves,
And struggles to burst forth into the light,
E'en so the soul within me hemmed and pent
Labored to burst its bonds and lose itself
In the surrounding and engulfing sea.
One awful throe of untold agony
Wrenched soul, and brain, and body at the last,
And then oblivion came. I knew no more.

When mind and sense returned, I was within
The sea-maid's bower beneath the sounding deep,
'Mid sweeter things than mortals dream of heaven.
One mighty wave of wondrous ecstasy
Filled soul and body,—and I woke to earth.

No human art can picture what I saw;
No human tongue can tell what I have known,
Or mind conceive it that has known it not;
But that brief moment in the siren's cell,
Those sounds my dreaming ears there listened to,
Those sights I saw, those feelings that were mine
Were almost worth eternities of pain.
And when I woke I wept to dream again.

Long Island, Me., Jan. 1st, 1886.

TOSSED ON THE TIDE.

Oh, the swift hours of the time that is nearing,
  Broad as the heavens and deep as the sea !
What, as they sweep on, to me are they bearing ?
  Lift up the veil of the future for me !

Out of eternity, into it going,
  Stopping not, staying not, years ever flee,
What on the tide of time's cycles onflowing,   ·
  Out of the darkness, is coming to me ?

I can but wait, whether surges surround me,
  Lashed by the tempests of sorrow and woe,
Or, in prosperity, rippling around me
  In pleasure's sunlight, they peacefully flow.

I cannot tell ! ·'Mid the flotsam and jetsam,
  Tide-tossed, dead men and wreck-splinters may lie,
Pearls and pink shells—happy is he who gets them
  Flung at his feet as the time-waves go by !

I cannot know ; but the current unsparing
  Something is bringing that eyes cannot see,
And on its bosom me, too, it is bearing
  On to a grave that is waiting for me.

Long Island, Me., April 7th, 1889.

THEN AND NOW.

Lap, lap, lap,
Slid the ripples along the beach
One day in the long ago,
Caressing each wave-worn stone,
And their silvery monotone
Seemed burdened with mystic speech.
With the tale that they seemed to tell,
I felt hope's ecstatic swell,
Hearing not in that ceaseless chord
The throb of woe.

Lap, lap, lap,
Glide the waves on the beach to-day
As they did in the long ago,
But joy in my breast is dead;
The peace of the past is fled,
Return now it never may;
And in ocean's vast chord sublime,
. Sounding on till the end of time,
Hope dwells not; I only hear
The throb of woe.

Long Island, Me., Feb. 13th, 1887.

A WINTER'S DAY.

The sunlight in golden gleaming
  Falls bright on the drifted snow,
Like a heavenly radiance streaming
  All over the world below.
Skies blue as in summer's brightness
  Smile down on a sea as blue,
While mantles of silvery whiteness
  The evergreens dark burst through.

A picture to men is given
  Unasked, and before them lies,
Fair, pure as the scenes of heaven
  Beheld by the angels' eyes ;
And as beautiful hues are blending,
  In the clear of the winter air,
As the tints in the world unending
  Which fields of the ransomed wear.

If things were as lovely ever
  As on this most perfect day,
How gladly would men forever
  In this beautiful, bright world stay !

But storms and corruptions center
  In the beautiful world we love,
So we turn where they never enter,
  To the lovelier land above.

Long Island, Me., Dec. 23rd, 1886.

DRIFTWOOD.

There's a ripple of shade on the ocean,
  With its gleaming expanse of blue,
Though a glitter of golden radiance falls
  The cloudless empyrean through,
And the shores of the grand old Atlantic rise
  Sun-kissed in each glorious hue.

There's a hint in the scene of beauty
  Of a horror that rests unsaid,
Strange, vague and nameless, that darkly hangs
  O'er the loveliness calm outspread,
Like a chilling blast from the world of souls,
  A message from some one dead.

It is only a broken splinter,
  Wave-worn, on the storm-vexed beach,
Yet what a tale of despair and death
  Could that sorrow-fraught fragment teach !
What memories of the past divulge,
  Had it sense and the power of speech !

For it came from a foundered vessel,
  Bitten deep by the ragged teeth
Of a sunken reef, that in ambush lay
  In a fleecy and foam-white wreath,
While the storm-winds howled and the breakers roared
  O'er the pitiless rocks beneath.

And the proud ship went to pieces
  And vanished forevermore,
While the wild waves swallowed the helpless crew
  And the hopes and plans she bore ;
And the only trace that remains to-day
  Is a splinter upon the shore,

And the heart-aches and bitter anguish
  Of the living who mourn the lost
Who sailed from home on the dancing waves
  That by them might ne'er be crossed,
Little dreaming soon on a wrathful tide
  Would their lifeless forms be tossed.

And this shivered and splintered timber
  Seems to tell of that horror still,
And the hopes and plans that were quenched for aye
  . When those hearts' hot blood grew chill.
Oh, a sad, sad thing on the lonely beach
  Is this mark of the tempest's will !

But far sadder are shattered fragments
  Tossed up by the sea of life,

That tell of hopes and ambitions high
  Ground up in its storm and strife,
All crippled and crushed by a cruel chance
  When misfortune's winds were rife.

For the heart that conceives a fancy
  Is torn when it comes to naught.
More bitter than death is a hope destroyed,
  Life's venture by shipwreck caught.
Better die than witness the loss of all
  While the soul is with feeling fraught.

So of all things, the saddest
  Are the wrecks on the shores of time,
Where the splinters of fleets we fondly launched,
  Our works that we deemed sublime,
All shattered, are flung by the tide of life
  At our feet as the billows chime.

For we feel that the fond hopes broken
  Are wrecks to us evermore ;
Our dearest dreams of delight destroyed,
  Driftwood on a sounding shore ;
Like the splinter flung on the lonely beach
  Where the waves of Atlantic roar.

Long Island, Me., April 29th, 1889.

OUT ON THE SEA.

    Out on the heaving sea
The dark clouds lower ; the thick mists hide the land
Where billows hiss and foam upon the strand ;
Through the dark shadows drives the rushing hail ;
Far flies the spray upon the howling gale ;
Darkness, destruction, chaos, blend to-night ;
Death is abroad in all his withering blight.
God pity men, whoever they may be,
      Out on the sounding sea !

    Down to the somber sea
No ray of starlight reaches ; all is dark,
And inky blackness wraps each struggling bark ;
From wrecks the waves are bearing men away,
While their last dirge the winds and waters play.
A thing of terror is a night like this,
For many a warm lip shall the surges kiss,
And many a mortal sink and cease to be,
      Out on the wrathful sea.

    Yet, on the changeful sea
The morrow's sun may shine out bright and clear,
All trace of nature's anger disappear,
Brightness and beauty rest upon the wave

In which to-night so many find a grave;
For nights of horror bring days clear and warm,
As storm e'er follows calm, and calm the storm.
Above the clouds will brightness ever be,
      And sometime reach the sea.

      Out on the sea of life
Are storm and darkness, wreck and blackest night,
And through the deep gloom shines no cheering light.
Some live the storm out, some are wrecked ere day,
And leave no ripple where they sink for aye;
Yet o'er the clouds do light and glory pour,
And those not whelmed shall greet their rays once more.
Heaven's radiance shall break through and calm the strife
      Of the great sea of life.

Long Island, Me., Dec. 24th, 1886.

DISAPPOINTED.

Cold blew the storm-wind from over the ocean,
　Darkly the clouds settled down on the sea,
Wild waves were rolling in ceaseless commotion,
　Flinging the spray high in air in their glee.
Lifeless and bare were the smooth, sandy reaches,
　Save for the sea-weed thrown up by the tide,
And the wreck-splinters strewn on the sea beaches,
　Scorned by the waves they no longer might ride.

Cold was the sea-shore on which I was sitting,
　Cold was my heart as I viewed the dark scene.
Gloomy my glances from wave to wave flitting
　As the bleak shore, the cold sky and sea green ;
Fitting the hour and the scene for my feeling,
　The darksome sky and the sea uncontrolled,
For disappointment life's brightness was stealing
　My heart, like the landscape, was gloomy and cold.

Changed is the weather, but not the old feeling,
　Changed is the time, but my heart is the same,
For disappointment's wounds are long in healing,
　The mind's sky cleared not when the earth's sky-change
　　　came ;

And, like old Ocean, whose waves are still swelling,
  Or like the rugged and storm-beaten shore,
My soul on crushed hopes forever is dwelling,
  Dark, cold and gloomy, unchanged evermore.

  . Port Republic, N. J., Nov. 22nd, 1885.

THE MYSTIC CURTAIN.

We stood together on a bare, cold hill,
My friend and I, while, in the broken west,
The orb of day was sinking to his death
Among the dark cloud-shadows.   Round about
The wind blew chill, and with its moaning voice
Betold the coming storm.   Far, far away,
The throbbing ocean sobbed aloud in woe,
Seeing the struggles of the drowning sun,
That faintly swam the damp and dismal rack
That choked his sinking, dying form in night.

We talked of many things upon the hill,
The happy, happy days forever past,
To come again no more ; the future hours,
Big with the promise of things yet to be,
Although they then were not ; ourselves, our hopes,
Our plans and fears ; and all the countless thoughts,
The "long, long thoughts" of youth came home to us,
As by us there the rising storm-wind sighed,
And clouds and darkness settled round about,
And daylight died.

And then, adown the hill,
My friend passed on and left me there alone.
I heard his footsteps ring upon the stones
As with firm tread he vanished ; and between
Myself and him the mists and shadows fell,
And all was dark.   A cloudy curtain dropped,'
And thus we were divided ; and the wind
Still louder moaned, and louder sobbed the sea
Upon the distant beaches hid from sight
By the same misty folds ;—and the sun set.

No thought prophetic stirred my inmost soul
With hint of what drew near, as from the hill
I wended homeward through the night alone.
Unseen, unrecognized, another veil
Had wrapped about my friend and hidden him.
Another curtain than the mist and cloud
Was falling in between him and myself,
The dark, strange .curtain that at some time drops
Behind each mortal, whose fringe scatters tears,
And pain, and heart-aches, and whose gloomy folds
Are waved and shaken by the breath of sighs
And moans of anguish.   This divided us,
Death's mantle dark :—we never met again.

Between us two that curtain hangs to-day
And hides him from my eyes, as on that night
The clouds and darkness shut him from my gaze.
I cannot see him, yet I know, afar,

Somewhere beyond the mists, the friend awaits
Who stepped into the shadows and was gone.
I may not raise the veil, at least not yet,
But some day will my hand the curtain lift
That us so long has parted.   I shall go
The path that my friend traveled years agone ;
I too shall know all there is yet to know ;
Into the shadows I shall also pass
From watching eyes, while just behind me falls
The mystic veil, and all the world grows dark,—
And the sun sets.

North Fayette, Me., March 23rd, 1888.

OVER THE WAVES.

Over the wavelets dancing bright,
   Out on their missions the white sails go,
Fair in the radiant autumn light,
   While sunbeams glitter and breezes blow.
The blue swells, flecked with the feathery foam
   Flung off by the sharp keels cleaving through,
Close in behind as they ride from home
   Underneath a glorious sky as blue.

Yet storms will come, and the waves roll high,
   That swell so gently around to-day,
And brave boats under their crests shall lie,
   That now so gallantly speed away.
But some bright harbors afar shall gain,
   Beyond my vision, I know not where,
Far over the treacherous, heaving main
   Now flashing, gleaming serenely fair.

I would that in one I might drift away
   From toil, and trouble, and vexing care,
Forever from all things around to-day,
   Away, I know not, I care not where!

It is perfect now, though a storm be near ;
  Then why prepare for the tempest's strife ?
Let it break unheeded !   I've more to fear
  From coming storms on the sea of life.

Long Island, Me., Sept. 15th, 1888.

SUICIDE.

Only a plunge in the dark, cold lake,
  'Neath the black and the murky sky,
To the sleep of death from which none awake,
Down under the ripples that curl and break
  As the storm-wind rushes by !

Only a leap from the bold steep shore,
  · In the dusk of the gloomy eve,
And the griefs and sorrows of earth are o'er,
Life's drama enacted forevermore,
  And the known shores of time I leave !

One leap, and the fever of life shall end
  In the shame of a suicide's death,
And the night of oblivion shall descend
On the hate of foe and the scorn of friend,
  With the last gasp of gurgling breath !

What a change from the glory of youth's bright morn
  Is its horrible, ghastly end !
From beauty and promise of life's fair dawn
To suicide's death and the harsh world's scorn !
  Light and dark threads of destiny blend.

I little thought in the days of youth
   That my bright dreams would come to this ;
That my visions of joy, and love, and truth
Would turn to sin and despair and ruth,
   And end in the cold wave's kiss.

To think of a being of flesh and blood,
   Once formed by the hand of God,
Lying low to rot on a bed of mud,
Preyed on by the fishes that swim the flood,
   By the worms and the shell-fish gnawed !

Or rising upward to float away,
   Once more in the sunlight bright,
Mutilated by creatures that round it play,
A horrible wreck in the light of day,
   A swollen and putrid sight !

'Tis a plunge from life and light into—what ?
   Into nothingness, heaven, or hell ?
Through the portal death's curtains forever shut,
The mystery of which the earth knoweth not,
   And which no soul comes back to tell.

Any fate is better than life of shame,
   Forsaken and shunned by all,
Sneered, scoffed at, taunted with ruined name,
Lost soul and body, deep stained in fame
   By a weak and a sinful fall !

Down, down to my death in the waters deep,
  'Neath the black and the ice-cold wave,
To lie in the slime where the foul worms creep,
And the hungry fishes around me sweep,
  I spring to a watery grave !

O, dark lake, take me and hide for aye
  From every mortal eye !
Conceal me closely from light of day !
Till time and eternity pass away
  Let me 'neath thy surface lie !

.O, roaring storm-wind, O, wild night-blast,
  For the last time I hear your dirge !
O, darkness, O, rain-cloud down-settling fast,
Good bye ! for my wrecked life is ever past !
  Enfold me, O, billowy surge !

Close o'er me, ye waters, and quench my life,
  And of my sad fate be dumb !
Farewell, ye elements' fitful strife,
With my soul's wild bitterness seeming rife !
  God, forgive ! Lake, receive me ! I come !

West Mount Vernon, Me., Aug. 4th, 1885.

WHOSE?

There's a glitter that lies on the water,
  There's a glimmer of gold on high,
As the sunbeams stream o'er the dancing waves
  From the depths of the dark blue sky ;
And the dimpling depths of ocean,
  The vault of the vast above,
Shine in warmth and beauty as bright as spring's
  'Neath the glowing sun's touch of love.

But under the smiling water
  Dead forms it has swallowed lie,
And the ghastly faces it blanched for aye
  With sightless eyes stare on high ;
And the blue of the sunlit heavens,
  So calmly, serenely fair,
Is cleft by the wings of the viewless shades
  Of the lost ones hovering there.

And this sunlight and warmth are fleeting,
  For winter approaches fast,
And the beauty that lies upon all to-day
  Is changing and cannot last.

The waters will rave in fury,
  The heavens will scowl on high,
Other dead eyes—whose ?—from the waves shall gaze,
  Other shades wing the darksome sky.

Portland, Me., Nov. 17th, 1888.

WITH THE TIDE.

I am floating down the river, drifting swiftly with the tide ;
On forever toward the ocean do the mighty waters glide,
And some time, though when I know not, I shall reach the
 boundless sea,
And I patiently am waiting till that blessed time shall be.

Sometimes clouds hang dark above me and the sky is over-
 cast,
But I feel that through the shadows will the sunlight break
 at last ;
And, though mists may gather round me, still I float upon
 my way,
For I know that just before me heaven's brightest sunbeams
 play.

Calmly, trustingly I'm drifting, though the way I cannot
 see,
For I know the shades, dividing, will disclose a course for
 me.
All upon this stream have floated, and, though it be wrapped
 in night,
I can enter where He entered, and shall find that all is
 right.

Though the sunlight smile around me or the skies above
     me lower,
Still I feel that I am nearer to the haven on the shore ;
For I know, somewhere before me, on the border of the sea,
There's a safe and quiet harbor opened wide to welcome
     me.

I am waiting till I reach it ; though it may be near or far,
Yet some time the tide will bear me safely o'er the harbor
     bar ;
Light will conquer gloom forever when I reach that haven
     blest ;
There some day, my drifting ended, I shall enter into rest.

   Port Republic, N. J., Feb. 9th, 1886.

UNDERCURRENT.

Dancing bubbles float on the surface
   With the hues of a rainbow bright,
But the dark, cold waters rush underneath
   In silent, resistless might.
Cloud-crests, by the sunbeams gilded,
   Dark, somber, float in mid-air ;
And, hidden under a lightsome guise,
   Oft rankles a deep despair.

Bright faces, the seeming gayest,
   Have sorrows concealed below,
And the fairest flowers in the fields of speech
   May bloom on a root of woe ;
And in every burst of music,
   Each thrilling and joyous strain,
The ears fine-strung catch an undertone,
   The throb of a hidden pain.

The laugh and the jest will circle,
   And the gleam of the smile go round,
While the world knows not of the smart concealed
   The sob in the laughter drowned ;

For sorrow and joy are sisters ;
   Only happiness oft appears
When the rippling rills of deceptive mirth
   Burst fresh from the fount of tears.

Long Island, Me., Jan. 9th, 1889.

DRIFTING.

I am drifting down the river,
  Ever drifting toward the sea,
Never stopping, never staying,
Onward still with no delaying,
Past the beacon lamps that quiver ;
  Drifting onward ceaselessly.

Never will the tide returning
  Bear me backward to the shore,
Whence I floated in the dawning
Of youth's bright and rosy morning ;
From it still, though for it yearning,
  I am drifting evermore.

It is on Time's restless river
  I am floating toward the sea ;
Past all known scenes quickly drifting,
  Under skies forever shifting ;
Present hours receding ever
  Drifting to futurity.

On from youth till life is ended
   Ebbs the tide that knows no flow ;
Sweeps the restless, rushing river,
At last whelming all forever ;
Over countless life-wrecks blended
   Still the mighty waters go.

Hurried onward with the rushing
   Of the current toward the sea,
Borne from much-loved scenes and places,
From the dear familiar faces,
Still I ride the waters gushing
   Onward to the great To-Be.

Graves of hopes and dead ambitions
   Line the shores by which I sweep,
Leaving loving friends forever,
Closest ties the currents sever,
Ever on with swift transitions
   To the boundless, roaring deep.

Not a helm to guide the motion
   Though the skies be overcast,
Though unknown the rocks surrounding,
Sand-bars, whirlpools, reefs abounding,
Helpless I drift toward the ocean,
   While the tempest gathers fast.

Wreck may come, for, darkly lying,
  Clouds and shadows wrap the wave.
In the future's misty distance,
Dangers beyond man's resistance
May o'erwhelm, and storm-winds flying,
  Howl a dirge above my grave.

Now I hear the breakers dashing,
  And I near the boundless sea !
Shores of Time are left forever !
All the ties of Living sever,
And I see the billows flashing
  In the vast Eternity !

Long Island, Me., Jan. 14th, 1885.

NIGHT BY THE SEASIDE.

I walked the shore 'mid the billows' roar,
  'Neath the black clouds whirled on high,
While the fine, sharp hail in the howling gale
  Went dashing and driving by.

The spray flew high to the stormy sky
  From the black and dripping rocks ;
Each wave's rebound with a thunder sound
  Told the power of the ocean-shocks.

The sharp sleet hissed through the driving mist
  As it plunged in the heaving sea,
And the green waves broke in a spumy smoke,
  That wild waves drove to lee.

I strained my sight through the falling night,
  Where the white-capped surges tore
By the rocks around with their foam-wreaths crowned,
  On their way to the snow-clad shore.

A dark shade gleamed where the brown weeds streamed,
  Like a sea-maid's floating hair ;
From its wild mates lost, a lone sea-bird tossed
  'Twixt the waves and the dusky air.

All the scene was rife with the fiercest strife
   When night settled o'er the main,
As, lashed by the hail and the roaring gale,
   The billows rolled back again.

Yet the war around, and the stunning sound,
   And the chaos of sea and air,
Left a calm behind in my restless mind
   And banished the thoughts of care.

The elements' fight on that stormy night
   Was awful, and yet sublime,
And that winter scene on the ocean green
   I shall think of in future time.

All things have changed since that beach I ranged ;
   That night will ne'er come again,
And nevermore shall I pace the shore
   With the thoughts that I cherished then.

That wild night blast is forever past,
   And memories only left ;
That time is fled and its moments dead,
   And the hopes I then had are reft.

Long Island, Me., Feb. 17th, 1885.

WRITTEN IN SAND.

Where the ripples break on the shining strand,
    On the quiet shore of an ocean bay,
Written deep in the silvery sand,
    The name of some thoughtless rambler lay.
Bold and firm was the writing fair,
    Every letter distinct and plain ;
Someone carelessly traced it there,
    Then wandered far from the spot again.

There lay the work of the idler's hand,
    Graven deep on the ocean shore,
Till a blue wave, kissing the shining sand,
    Left it as smooth as it was before.
Many are striving to write their name
    Where the waves of time will forever flow,
And trying to build for themselves a fame
    To last while the ages shall come and go.

Thus kings and princes their names engrave
    On the sands of time ere they pass away ;
The shore is swept by oblivion's wave,
    And their work is gone from the world for aye.

Thus poets and painters will strive to win
   A deathless fame that shall always last, ·
But the restless waves of time rolling in
   Soon bear them into forgotten past.

The soldier writes with his bloody hand
   His name in letters both bold and clear ;
The surf of forgetfulness sweeps the strand,
   And the name of the hero must disappear.
And all who strive for a deathless fame,
   A record to last while the world shall stand,
Are only trying to write their name
   On a changing tablet of shifting sand.

And this is the value of earth's renown ;
   The rich and mighty, the proud and great,
Their names and actions are writing down
   To be swept away by remorseless fate.
The proudest record the world can show
   Is but a record inscribed in sand,
Eternity's waves, in their ceaseless flow,
   Will smooth forever time's changing strand.

North Fayette, Me., Jan. 10th, 1883.

WOODLAND WHISPERS.

LITTLE SWEETHEARTS.

Over my memory softly are stealing
   Thoughts of a day in the bright, happy past,
And a half-pleasant, half-sorrowful feeling
   From the moist eye bids the tears trickle fast.
Fondly I think of a day gone forever;   '
   Of what has been but can nevermore be;
And in my dreams and my reveries ever,
   From the dead past comes this picture to me:

Two little sweethearts with bright, happy faces,
   On a fresh hillside where strawberries grow,
Plucking the red fruit from green hiding-places,
   Lightsome and free as the breezes that blow.
Fair is the face of the bright little maiden,
   Hair like the sunbeams and eyes like the sky,
Lips smiling over the basket fruit-laden,
   And the boy walking beside her is —— I.

Children we were when we wandered together,
   With our hearts filled with a warm, childish love,
Calm and serene as the bright summer weather,
   Pure as the skies that were arching above.

But I soon lost my sweet hope and my treasure ;
   Joys that I dreamed of will ne'er be my own,
For the bright presence that made life a pleasure
   Left me to tread in the dark pathway alone.

No more to me come the hopes that then found me,
   On that bright day in the dim long ago.
All the pure joys that then clustered around me
   Soon were swept from me by time in its flow.
Now, with hair whitened by hours in their flying,
   Sadly I wander life's desert alone ;
My little sweetheart has long years been lying
   In her last rest 'neath the moss-covered stone.

Port Republic, N. J., Jan. 21st, 1886.

WOODLAND WHISPERS.

The boughs of the woodland arches thrill at the touch of
the unseen breeze,
And a whisper runs through the cool arcades of the verdant
and murmuring trees,
And the trembling spruce, and the hemlock dark, and the
slim fir's tapering spire
Join in the song of the beech and birch to the white pine's
quivering lyre.

Perchance there are souls in the woodland kings rooted
deep in the moldering ground,
And the ancient monarchs, chained fast so long, sigh softly
their woes profound,
Sad histories of a past long dead, vainly striving men's
hearts to teach,
Breathing thoughts and feelings of other days in a half-
articulate speech.

Or the fairies and dryads may haunt them still, as they did
in the years of old,
Their voices blending in low, sad chime as they sigh for
those moments told,
And the golden days when they reigned alone in the leafy,
bewildering ways,
Ere Mammon-worship and skeptic doubt invaded their
ancient maze.

But the woodland whispers, those forest hymns, are thrill-
    ing with mystic speech,
Unknown, unnoticed by sordid hearts ; the poet's alone
    they reach ;
And even he with the tuneful lips, with his dreaming and
    fine-strung soul,
Comprehends but part of the wondrous tale ; no mortal
    may know the whole.

'Tis a privilege to the Muses' sons to visit the sacred
    ground,
Where, leaf-crowned monuments of the past, the great
    trees tower around.
With their murmuring echoes a peace profound will enter
    the restless mind,
And the soothing voices, half-understood, their tenderness
    leave behind.

And a sweet and a holy task it is grand symphonies to
    translate
From the forest language to mortal speech ; how pleasing,
    and yet how great !
For the thoughts half caught, and the songs half heard,
    and the mysteries half made plain
By the woodland whispers half-understood, fairy voices
    repeat in vain.

Nature, grand, inspired, the poetic source, blame not if
    the strain be weak,
For even poets can catch but part that her nymphs of the
    woodland speak.
Beauty, grandeur, tenderness, all are there, go listen and
    you will hear
What human language and human bards are powerless to
    render clear.

North Fayette, Me., Aug. 10th, 1889.

ALONE WITH NATURE.

You who are harrassed by the cares of life,
Confused by turmoil, overcome by grief,
Wearied by labor and weighed down by pain,
Uuntil the language of the Great Supreme
Becomes unknown to you, forsake the world
Of bustling, busy striving after wealth,
And stand alone with Nature.   There will come
Home to your heart an overpowering sense
Of a vast, wonderful Intelligence,
That underlies and rules all Nature's works,
Governs all things by wise and fixed decrees,
And for the best ; — save where its peaceful law
Is turned aside by reckless, willful man.

Go, stand, as I have stood, before a storm,
And see the ragged, night-black clouds rush on
Upon the howling gale, until the sun
Is blotted out of heaven and all is gloom ;
Gaze on the grove of silver birches tall,
Slender and pliant, in their robes of green,
And see them rock and sway in rhythmic grace

Before the hurricane that bows them down ;
See them swing back and forth in mystic dance,
In unison with the deep monotone
Of the oncoming storm, the roaring gale,
The rippling patter of the first great drops
From the black cloud, and with the thunder's bass,
To the great orchestra, while o'er the scène
The lightning flashes its electric torch ;
And if the sight beget in you no thought
Of some Supreme that rules it and directs,
If the grand harmony the tempest plays
Suggest not to your mind some Power beyond
And far excelling feeble human thought,
Then is the soul within you numbed and dead.

Go look at eventide, as I have looked,
Upon some bright lake, gleaming like a shield
Of polished silver in the mellow light
That waits on sunset.   See its surface clear,
Unrippled by a single dimpling breeze,
Throwing back perfect pictures of the woods
That line its shores and blaze in autumn hues ;
Not such, dull shades as early frosts produce,
But glorious colors that October suns
Bring to the ripened foliage, gorgeous tints
Of scarlet, yellow, amber, russet, gold,
Brown, buff and crimson, mingled with the green
Of pine and hemlock, blended with a skill

Alone with Nature.

And harmony no mortal artist e'er
Had power to copy.   And more, add to this
The bright reflections of a few soft clouds   .
Floating above, in skies as blue and clear
As maiden's eyes of innocence and truth,
With borders flushed and gilded by the glance
Still cast upon them by the hidden sun.
Soften the glowing picture by the shades
Of quiet coves and bare rocks, dark and bold,
And silvery places where no image rests,
And, as you gaze upon the beauteous scene,
If you then feel not a peace, sweet, divine,
And almost know the thoughts of Nature's heart,
Then is your soul a callous one indeed.

Flee to the woods in summer's brightest days,
And lie upon the cool earth strewn with leaves,
And fallen needles that a year now dead
Plucked from the arrowy pines, that tower above,
Like giant fingers, mutely pointing out
The land of rest that waits the weary soul,
And listen to the cadence of the breeze
Murmuring in music through the dark green boughs
That wave and toss a hundred feet on high,
Mingled with bursts of untaught melody
From countless birdlings hidden in the trees.   ·
See the bright sunshine glint and glance in gold,
As through the limbs the gentle zephyrs move,

In changeful quiverings to the earth below,
And sensibilities are blunt indeed,
That, drinking in the grand old forest hymn
In all its soothing changes, feel no hint
Of something more than chance that does it all,
And pours into the heart its restfulness.

Or stand upon some rocky headland bold,
That gores old ocean's side, when winter's storms
Are thundering around.   List to the roar
Of mighty waves that beat upon the strand
With force that jars and shakes the solid earth.
See the white spray fly mountain-high above
The wet, black rocks the sea attacks in vain ;
See the wild billows climb, and slip, and slide
Round the rough cliffs that hurl them back again
Upon those close behind, that still rush on ·
In mad succession to the snow-clad shore,
While sleet-balls dart down from the bursting clouds,
Hissing into the boiling sea below,
Whose foam-flecked waters whelm them as they fall.
Watch the lone sea-bird toss upon the tide
Between the green waves and the inky air,
Exulting in the chaos all around.
View the dark kelp and rock-weed stream afar
On ocean's throbbing bosom, while beneath
Great Nature's heart heaves with the heaving sea,
And from the madly warring elements,

The lesson of their one vast secret learn,
The one fact that all nature fain would teach :
It was not chance that fashioned all things thus.

Go, then, when weary, worn and broken down
In mind or body, far away from man,
And walk alone with Nature.   Face to face
With her commune, and gain her peace and rest.
No matter when or where you seek her side,
There's beauty wheresoe'er she can be found,
At whatsoever time,   Through ear and eye
She pours her rest and beauty to the soul,
And cares and troubles vanish.   Let her breathe
Into the inmost spirit God's own peace.
Filled with that peace and beauty, turn again
And face once more the care and toil of life,
With health and strength renewed and courage fresh
And manfully press onward to the gate
That leads to the Hereafter.   Treasure up
And store away within your inmost heart
The silent sermon that all souls might feel,
And, bettered for this life and that to come,
Thank God with Nature 'you have been alone.

Long Island, Me., Jan. 15th, 1887.

NATURE'S MUSIC.

Nature, thy great heart with music is throbbing;
   In all thy changes thy melodies dwell,
From fairy murmurs of light summer hours
   To the grand chords of the tempest's wild swell;
And to the soul-harp in unison with thee
   All tones unite in a chorus complete;
All thy sounds blend in a grand, changing anthem,
   All thy notes melt into harmonies sweet.

Teach me the wonderful music, O, Nature,
   Breathed by the numberless children of thine;
Teach me the wild and sweet song of the birdling
   Hanging a-swing on its nest in the vine;
Teach me the deep, solemn chant of the ocean
   Rolling its waves on its margin of sand
In its calm moments, and, roused by the tempest,
   The wondrous swell of its melody grand.

Teach me the soothing tune in the low murmur
   Of the light zephyr, sweet minstrel of thine,
Breathing its soul in musical cadence
   To the soft notes of the harp of the pine;
Teach me the rippling and silvery music
   Of the streams coursing thy valleys along,
The quick tattoo of the midsummer shower,
   The thunder's bass to thy soul-stirring song.

Sing to me ever, O, great voice of Nature,
    Soothe me with all of thy numberless chords ;
Whate'er thy mood, there is harmony ever
    In all the sounds which thy kingdom affords.
Breathe on my spirit, the soul-harp so wondrous;
    Set in vibration each quivering string ;
Let the grand psalm throb forever within me,
    While in accord all thy melodies ring. ·

Port Republic, N. J., Oct. 10th, 1886.

BLASTED.

A pine-tree king of the forest stood
  And basked in the light serene,
High rearing above all its brotherhood
  Its dark tower of glossy green.

A man stood high in the human throng,
  A king of the sons of men
By right of mind and a genius strong,
  The power of the tongue and pen.

But storm-clouds gathered above the tree,
  And the lightning's finger of flame
Touched its leafy crest and it ceased to be,
  Save the wreck of a giant frame.

And passion breathed with its blasting breath,
  The blight of its hot desire;
The strong man sank to the caves of death
  At the touch of its finger of fire.

All that marks the tree as the years roll on
  Is a stump in the crumbling ground,
And every trace of the man is gone,
  Save a moldering churchyard mound.

North Wayne, Me., Nov. 10th, 1887.

MAPLE LEAVES.

Once again the leaves are turning
  On the lofty maple trees,
And their banners bright and burning
  Wave upon the autumn breeze.
Scarlet, crimson, brown and yellow
  Hues on every hand appear,
Soon to sober tints to mellow,
  Dying with the dying year.

All too soon is summer ended,
  And the summer's light and bloom;
All too soon these glories, blended,
  Sere and dead, in winter's tomb,
The boughs will leave undefended,
  That so brilliantly now wave,
And, their autumn splendor ended,
  Sink forgotten to the grave.

Brightest scenes are ever fleetest,
  Fairest flowers soonest die,
Shortest hours are ever sweetest,
  Richest hues the soonest fly.
Frosts destroy the leaves of summer
  And the buds we hold so dear,
And that swift and silent comer,
  Death, life's frost, is ever near.

'Tis not strange those flaming glories
  Sadden and subdue the heart,
For how many dear life-stories
  Close when summer hours depart!
Many leave our side forever
  When the maple's sere leaves fall.
'Tis not strange that dead leaves ever
  Bring to mind the shroud and pall.

Meet it is that hours of sadness
  Come with autumn's gorgeous hues,
And those tints of light and gladness
  Dim, funeral thoughts infuse;
For those leaves so bright and fleeting
  Soon will flutter, dark and sere,
O'er the tombs of hearts now beating
  And the cold grave of the year.

Port Republic, N. J., Sept. 20th, 1885.

THE MOON AND THE FIREFLY.

Down in the grass where the daisies slept
  While the pearly dewdrops gleamed around,
From blade to blossom a fire-fly crept
  Like a living spark on the dark, cool ground.

Humble the spot where the insect dwelt,
  And of little use all that he could do,
Yet well contented the small one felt
  If his faint light flickered the whole night through.

But high in the heavens the full moon rode,
  And her wondrous radiance shone around,
And the pale, cold splendor that from her flowed,
  The faint, fair light of the fire-fly drowned.

Abashed, the insect then crept away
  Deep under the grasses and flowerets wild,
But the moon's light sought him out where he lay,
  And her pale, fair face on the fire-fly smiled.

Of his humble duty he thought no more,
  For his tiny being was filled with love,
And he cared not to shine as he had before,
  For he saw but the white moon that shone above.

Lured on by her cold and beautiful smile,
  He followed along till the dawn of day,
With a wearying pinion, for many a mile,
  Till weak and helpless at last he lay.

And there in the cold, dim morning air,
  With wings all broken and drenched in dew,
He lay and expired in his deep dispair,
  While the cold moon swept from his dying view.

Affections placed on one far above
  The rank of the lover, however true,
Will yield but the pang of rejected love,
  As its cherished object recedes from view.

With a cold and pitiless smile will set
  The moon that wins true though but humble love,
And the breaking heart and the eyelids wet
  Repay the worship of things above.

Long Island, Me., Jan. 24th, 1885.

IN THE HAMMOCK.

Overhead the green leaves quiver,
 Shaken by the viewless breeze ;
Underneath the grasses shiver
 In the shadow of the trees ;
In the air are murmurs flying,
Rising, sinking, swelling, dying,
With the light winds changing ever
 Their soft, airy melodies.

Overhead the sunlight glances
 In among the treetops tall ;
Underneath the brightness dances
 Where the cool, dark shadows fall ;
Checkered lights and shadows changing
As winds through the boughs are ranging,
Bring a thousand airy fancies,
 And day-dreams the breezes call.

The heart quivers like the grasses,
 Or the green leaves overhead,
When across its fibers passes
 Throb of joy, or pain, or dread ;
And all souls must thrill forever,
For the breath of passion never
Fails to sweep them, and all classes
 Change from mirth to grief instead.

Life is changing as the sighing
  Of the wind among the trees ;
Hopes and fears are rising, dying,
  Like the fitful summer breeze ;
And our heart-tones, never ending,
Sad and joyous, ever blending,
Shouts of mirth and bitter crying,
  Chord in life's strange harmonies.

Lights of joy and shades of sorrow
  Mingle on its onward way,
And the shining of to-morrow
  Blends with shading of to-day,
Till life's mighty picture finished
Glows in splendor undiminished
'Neath God's eye, and seems to borrow
  Beauty from the shadows' play.

North Fayette, Me., Aug. 18th, 1885.

TOUCHED BY THE FROST.

One by one the flowers fade
  At evening's chilly breath,
Withering in forest shade
  To their autumnal death ;
And one by one their hues are lost,
    Touched by the frost.

One by one the bright leaves fall
  Down from the parent trees.
Sere and dead, like autumn's pall,
  They rustle in the breeze,
As to the cold earth they are tossed,
    Touched by the frost.

One by one the hopes decay
  That we have cherished long,
As disappointment in their way
  Breathes icily and strong.
-They perish when their paths are crossed,
    Touched by the frost.

One by one the friends depart
  Whose lives were bound to ours;
Death breathes on each loving heart,
  And, like leaves, hopes and flowers,
They leave us, and we mourn them lost,
    Touched by the frost.

One by one the days go by
  To swell the tide of years
And, sweet or sad, the moments fly
  That bring us smiles or tears.
We, too, shall sink, like leaves wind-tossed,
    Touched by the frost.

North Fayette, Me., Oct. 29th, 1884.

FROM BOTH SIDES.

The pure snow crystal that the skies give birth,
    Falling, viewed from below, looks dark as night,
But seen when resting on the lap of earth
    It gleams in beauty of a dazzling white.

The self-same water in the shadowed pool
    Shows inky black to those who wander near,
That the bold diver in its bosom cool
    Looks up and sees a silver white and clear.

The thunder-cloud, above a sable pall
    Rolling its jetty volume fold on fold,
Sweeps over, and the sunlight changes all
    To fleecy billows edged with red and gold,

All things wear hues unlike to unlike eyes,
    And other standpoints other forms will show;
Their shape and shade depend on where they rise;
    Not from one view may man their nature know.

Call not a single act ill-done, or well;
    Motives alone could give an honest light.
Call no heart good or bad, for none can tell;
    Since to no two is man the selfsame sight.

Long Island, Me., Feb. 1st, 1889.

SONGS OF SORROW.

CONFESSIONS.

Come hither, my fair, sweet maiden,
  With the tender and questioning eyes,
Half-way betwixt child and woman,
  When the strange, new thoughts arise,
And the dawn of a glorious promise
  Seems to break in the future's skies.

Come hither, my innocent girlie,
  Fresh as just from the Hand above,
Whose young heart is vaguely thrilling
  With the prelude of coming love,
In a dream-world whose disappointment,
  Sin, and sorrow you yet must prove.

Let your pure lips fashion the questions
  In your dewy eyes I see,
Though buried and sad recollections
  Laid bare by your words may be;
For I know that you long to fathom
  Why the years have dealt thus with me;

And why, in this world of beauty,
  Where joy only you have known,
A sadness is ever upon me,
  That deeper with years has grown ;
And why, amid love and sunshine,
  I am gray, and wrinkled, and lone.

Ah, Bessie, it seems so lately,   .
  Though years have passed by since then,
That I, too, was young and buoyant,
  Hoping, planning, like all young men,
With my life's skies, like yours, all glowing, —
  Now never to clear again !

Yes ; it seems only yester-evening,
  Though so many long years ago,
That a full-orbed moon came sailing
  Up the heavens, serene and slow,
Till the gold-spangled sky's vast azure
  Was flooded with silvery glow ;

And one tree-bordered lane was silent,
  Deserted one village street
Whose shadows the far-off lamp-posts
  And moonlight made more complete,
While a cool night breeze went stealing
  Through the spring-blooms dewy-sweet.

And down through its grand, dim archway,
  So purely and peacefully still,
While the dusk and the springtime fragrance
  Hovered soft o'er the tree-crowned hill,
Four happy young hearts moved onward
  To the old, ruined Blackman Mill.

They passed through a yawning doorway,
  Like a vast and a sightless eye,
Staring black up the street so silent,
  While the wind and the stream stole by,
And in fancy again we enter,
  Ben, Madge, and Annie and I.

Through the power of a fond remembrance
  Again on that scene I gaze ;
Open doorways and shattered windows,
  Shot through by the moon's white rays ;
Black holes in the rude floor, gaping
  Like the gates into demon ways.

And the saw-frames stood like specters
  Of the laborers there no more,
As we picked our way in the darkness
  Round the timbers that strewed the floor,
To the open end of the ruin
  O'erhanging the stream and shore.

The moonlight fell on the water,
  Chiming onward through shade and shine,
Till it glowed in the tender glory,
  A lake for a world divine ;
And the scent-laden wind sang ever
  Through the boughs of poplar and pine.

The golden stars' faint reflections
  Twinkled up from the shimmering plain
To where heaven's lamps celestial,
  Like calm eyes, looked down again
On that silvery mirror, girdled
  With a tree-belt's shadowy chain.

'Twas a landscape let down from heaven
  In an evening of Paradise ;
Nothing like it, I know, will ever
  Be seen by my waking eyes ;
In a setting of memories tender
  That hour, like a jewel, lies.

What we said and dreamed I know not,
  But many a tender thought,
And hope, and plan there cherished,
  With happiness deeply fraught,
The years have fulfilled for others,
  While with me they came to naught.

The evening changed into dawning ;
  The dawning grew into day ;
Years passed.   Ben and Madge are married,
  But further I can not say ;
And Annie sleeps in the churchyard
  By that shaded street far away.

And I — I am what you see me,
  Gray, wrinkled, lonely and old ;
That scene, those hopes can return not
  Till the jasper gates unfold.
Little girl, your story's beginning,
  But mine is a tale that's told.

Leave the old man his sorrow, Bessie ;
  Your tender young eyes are wet ;
God grant that your sun in shadows
  And sorrow may never set
Like mine !   But its rising beauties
  I nevermore can forget.

North Fayette, Me., July 28th, 1889.

THE PATRIARCH'S DEATH.

The old man sat alone at eventide,
At rest from all his labors ; day by day,
For weeks and months, his strength had ebbed and failed,
His thin, white locks grown thinner, and his beard,
His silver beard, had turned a purer snow ;
His once large form grown shrunken, and the lines
Of age and care sunk deeper in his face,
For he was full of years and goodly works.

His friends and he alike knew that the hour
Of final separation neared apace,
But all was peace with him.   Behind him lay
A long and useful life, almost complete,
The good fight fought, the faith well kept, the course
Finished at last, the work done given him,
And all his duty, as to him made plain,
To God and man, as far as in him was.

Content to go, and in his faith secure,
Calmly he waited for the summons home,
The message from his Father ; trusting still
His work might gain for him the plaudit sweet,
The blest reward, the welcome words, " Well done ! "

And as he sat then in the twilight hour,
The gloaming of the day and of his life,
An angel's finger touched the beating heart,
And it grew still forever.   In his chair
A waxen image leaned, a look of peace
Upon the calm, still features.   Gone the lines
Of age and care; some unseen, loving hand
Had smoothed them all away. • The silver crown
Of scanty locks, and snowy, floating beard
Gleamed like a halo round the face serene,
Where a still beauty and calm majesty
In grandeur sat; but he, the father loved,
The friend respected through a godly life,
He, who had striven, suffered, fought, and won,
Was gone forever to his sure reward;
His God had taken him.

   West Mt. Vernon, Me., July 23rd, 1888.

DREAM AND REALITY.

The farmer stood by the cottage door,
  When the summer day was done,
As down from the hillside the cattle came
  To the farm-yard, one by one,
And, following close to the sleek-haired kine,
  Came the farmer's only son.

The father gazed on the manly boy
  With his heart full of love and pride,
And thought in the days when life's toil was done,
  And he neared the stream's dark side,
That loving and filial hands would smooth
  His path down to death's cold tide.

He dreamed of life's evening calm and sweet,
  When the boy should come home to stay,
And he should stand, as he stood that night,
  A grandsire old and gray,
While his son's son followed the cattle home
  At the close of the summer day.

But the years rolled on, and those bright dreams fled;
   They vanished in tears and pain ;
For the son sleeps under the golden sands
   Of a Californian plain,
And the old man drives home the cows alone
   On the rock-ribbed hills of Maine.

South Fayette, Me., June 1st, 1887.

O, FAIR AND SPOTLESS SLEEPER!

O, fair and spotless sleeper, calm, serene,
   With lovely lips still parted as for breath,
And sweet eyes, hidden by a snowy screen,
   Locked in the marble mystery of death !
O, blameless one upon a sin-stained earth !
   O, stainless soul amid a thousand crimes !
Pure as in infancy, the heavenly birth
   But ushers you, unchanged, to fairer climes.

O, waxen image of white purity !
   O, sculptured form of marble innocence !
You are not like one from earth just set free,
   In pity called from suffering intense ;
You seem a new creation of God's hand,
   Fresh formed in rare and perfect loveliness,
Awaiting life by His divine command,
   Not one that death has freed from her distress.

The happiness that endlessly endures
   Has dawned for you, and griefs and cares are done ;
The beauties of the world beyond are yours ;
   The glories of eternal life are won.
Unseal those icy lips of frozen clay,
   Seeming no mortal maiden's, but divine,
Tell what those earth-dulled ears have heard to-day,
   What those veiled eyes have seen since meeting mine.

In vain !   Death's secret you may not reveal,
    Although the vast, stupendous change you know ;
The faint gleams that across your features steal
    Are all the answer I may hope below ;
Those dim reflections of the light above,
    That o'er your pale and perfect beauty play,
Are a reply, and now I leave you, love ;
    I, too, shall follow on and learn — some day.

Long Island, Me., Nov. 16th, 1889.

MEMORIES.

It is only a line of a sacred song, an air of the long
    ago,
Flung off on the breeze by the fresh young lips that carol
    unthinking why ;
But the singer trilling those tuneful notes knows not, and
    she cannot know,
With the melody comes to one heart a throb, a tear-drop
    to one sad eye.

Is is not the tune, though a tender one, that summons the
    falling tear ;
Nor the words it bears, though they, too, are sweet, there
    are many as sweet as they ;
Nor the fair young singer, though pure and true is the
    maid with the voice so clear,
That fills my heart with a silent pain at the close of the
    long, bright day.

I think of the one I last heard breathe that air in the years
gone by,
And an empty place in my inmost soul mourns a singer
that sings no more.
But nothing ever that void can fill, for those lips in the
churchyard lie,
And the spirit they served then carols now on another and
fairer shore.

North Fayette, Me., Aug. 6th, 1889.

GONE.

You have gone and left us.   We see no more
   The smile we had learned to cherish.
The form we loved has been laid away
Beneath the sod till the judgment day,
And the soul has flown to the better shore
   Where the things we love ne'er shall perish.

You are gone from us and our love, for aye,
   To the land where we mortals go not,
Beyond earth's trials, beyond its cares,
Beyond our fears and beyond our prayers,
Beyond the stars and the gates of day,
   To a life that as yet we know not.

Your feet so tender have passed along,
   Outstripping our own that linger.
They have gone the road that our souls shall know,
The long, long journey we too must go ;
You have followed into the world of song
   The death-angel's beckoning finger.

The sins of earth you will never know;
  From the right you will never wander.
You will ne'er, like us, sink in woe and tears;
You are safe at home for eternal years;
It is well with you, but we miss you so,
  Since you passed to the land up yonder!

Farewell!   No more shall we see your face,
  And our sorrowing hearts are aching;
But the weary waiting will soon be o'er;
We shall meet again on a heavenly shore,
Where tears and partings can have no place,
  When eternity's morn is breaking.

Long Island, Me., Feb. 22nd, 1888.

THE GRAVEYARD BY THE SHORE.

Oh, the glowing summer weather,
When we wandered forth together,
Hearts as light as downy feather,
　To the graveyard by the shore !
While we passed, in sunlight glancing
Golden butterflies went dancing,
And the bird-songs thrilled entrancing,
　In the yore, yes ; in the yore.

Crumbling headstones old and hoary
Told in vain the solemn story
Of those gathered home to glory,
　Entered in at Heaven's door ;
For the pallid pillars, gleaming
In the sunlight. o'er them streaming
Joy, not sorrow, told, in seeming
　Nothing more, no ; nothing more

What to us, whose hearts were leaping,
Were the dead around us sleeping ?
Our eyes found no cause for weeping
　In those gravestones old and hoar.
Birds, aud butterflies, and flowers,
Health and happiness were ours,
Life and love in rosy bowers
　Lay before us, close before.

Ah ! that day is gone forever !
Soon our life-paths had to sever,
And since then my feet have never
    Trod that graveyard by the shore.
Years have flown, some six or seven,
Still those pillars point to heaven,
But I'll see day change to even
    By them never, nevermore !

Birds still sing in tuneful numbers
O'er those quiet, dreamless slumbers,
And the butterfly encumbers
    The bud there as in the yore ;
But my life is changed forever,
Since our spirits had to sever,
And now, I shall see her never,
    Nevermore, no ; nevermore.

Far away my course is shifted,
Love out of my life has drifted,
And a weight ne'er to be lifted
    Crushes me, unknown of yore.
From that graveyard I have tarried,
But my darling since they carried,
Sleeping, back, and left her buried
    ·Evermore, yes ; evermore.

North Fayette, Me., Sept. 6th, 1889.

CALM AFTER STORM.

·Afflictions may roll like the waves of the ocean,
   And storm-clouds of sorrow life's skies overcast,
But some time will end all earths's grief and commotion;
   The sorest of trials is over at last.

Sad moments will come, and there is no escaping,
   For none may evade the all-chastening hand
Which, every destiny perfectly shaping,
   Blends shining and shading in harmony grand.

Though cares of the world and the sorrows of living,
   Its pains and afflictions must heavily fall,
'Tis only to wait what the future is giving,
   And peace and sweet rest softly cover them all.

The tears of the mourner fall fast in the shadows,
   And weeping endures till the fleeting of night;
Hope's day-star will rise with the dawn o'er the meadows,
   And happiness come with the coming of light.

Time softens all sorrow, but, oh! it is bitter,
   The parting that lasts evermore upon earth,
Even though the bright rainbow of promise may glitter,
   The hope of reunion by heavenly birth!

Rest cometh at last.   From an all-loving Giver
  The calm waves of peace to the weary heart roll ;
Sorrow's dark stains shall all be washed white in the river
  Whose life-giving current transfigures the soul.

Long Island, Me., Feb. 13th, 1889.

SHOWERS.

The raindrops are heavily falling,
  They rest on the blades of the grass ;
The sunlight and blue skies are hidden
  By the dark clouds that gloomily pass ;
But brightness will follow the shower,
  The sun shine serenely again,
And the whole earth be purer and fairer,
  Beautified by the generous rain.

Sorrow's tear-drops are heavily falling,
  Gloomy thoughts shroud the joy in the heart,
And darkness and dreary forebodings
  Quench the brightness Hope fain would impart ;
But the shadows will roll from the pathway,
  The dark clouds above it will rise,
And all things be purer and fairer
  For the tear-drops that fall from the eyes.

West Mt. Vernon, Me., July 19th, 1886.

ISOBELLE.

Isobelle !   My first and last,
In the darkness I am keeping
Sleepless watch in lonely weeping,
    Ever dreaming of the past,
Of a face than angel's fairer,
Of the maiden truer, rarer
    Than this sin-stained earth can claim.
Seraph for a season given,
Lent a little while from heaven,
Holy heart in spotless mortal,
    Soon set free from sin and shame,
You have passed the silent portal,
From this life to that immortal,
    And grief's billows round me swell,
        Isobelle !

Isobelle !   My life, my all,
Once your tender presence blessed me,
Once your loving hands caressed me,
    Now for you I vainly call !
Now my heart is sad and lonely,
My arms clasp the shadows only,
    And your face no more I see !

For your love I vainly languish;
Vainly calls my soul in anguish
From earth's sorrow-shadowed places,
   For you do not come to me!
Mine no more are your embraces!
Grave-grass grows between our faces,
   And your love you can not tell,
        Isobelle!

Isobelle! My lost and prized,
Loved while yet in earthly station
With an angel's adoration,
   When you passed but recognized,
Death has cruelly bereft me;
Only memories are left me,
   And the sobs of sorrow swell!
Never mine the dreamed-of blisses,
Mine no more your tender kisses,
But your sweet name's liquid falling
   Is my music, Isobelle!
O, white soul in joys enthralling,
Hear the hungry heart that's calling
   From the shadows where I dwell,
        Isobelle!

Isobelle! My love, my love!
Can you hear my bitter crying
In the gloom where I am lying?
   Can you see me from above?

Is your soul affection-laden
As on earth, O, seraph maiden,
 Safe beyond the golden gate?
Do you linger, praying ever,
Just beyond the rolling river?
With God's glory round you lying
 For me do you fondly wait?
O my lost one, hear my crying!
Mine in living, mine in dying,
 In Eternity as well,
  Isobelle!

Isobelle! O, Isobelle!
As on earth, now up above me,
Guide me, guard me, lead me, love me,
 Till Death's waters round me swell!
Silently your earth-life bade me
Shun the wrong, and better made me;
 May its power still be seen!.
I am nobler, purer, truer
For a love that will endure.
Though the dark and silent river
 Pour its torrents in between!
Souls will sunder, spirits sever,
Yet it can not be forever;
 I shall join you where you dwell,
  Isobelle!

North Fayette, Me., Dec. 28th, 1889.

THE UNION STATION.

I have often sat in that room so vast,
　While trains unheeded went thundering by,
Alone, with a multitude hurrying past,
　And numberless strangers lingering nigh.

They come and go, and they shift and change;
　They cross and recross the echoing floor,
In a varying vision of features strange,
　Winding in and out through each open door.

And again and again, as I watch the scene,
　All types of humanity hurrying past,
My mind flies backward to what has been,
　While a shadow is over my spirit cast.

Some look familiar recalls one dear,
　The face that I loved in years gone by,
And I dream for an instant that it is near,
　When that of some stranger meets my eye.

Some glance or gesture, some trick of dress,
　Some form or feature I seem to know,
Once more brings a vision of loveliness '
　From the gathered shadows of long ago.

Too often, while watching the varying stream
    That is ever eddying round the door,
A fancied resemblance recalls the dream,
    And I look for a loved one that comes no more.

In some vacant chamber within my heart,
    Some ghostly hall of the haunted past,
Will a throbbing sorrow re-echoing start,
    As the footsteps ring through the station vast.

But she never crosses the sounding floor,
    Though many reminding of her I see ;
She has entered the last station's sheltering door,
    Golden-bright on the inside, but dark to me.

No train returning will bear her back
    To earth's way-station, but I can wait ;
For Time's car is bearing me down the track
    To the heavenly terminus' glittering gate.

North Fayette, Me., Dec. 24th, 1889.

THE HOLLY QUEEN.

A picture is spread before me of a maiden serene and
  fair,
With eyes like the skies of summer and its light in her
  golden hair.
'Tis the herald of Merry Christmas, the beautiful Holly
  Queen,
With her head crowned and arms o'erflowing with glisten-
  ing leaves of green.

It brings back another picture from the days of long
  ago,
The face of another maiden, with her cheeks and her eyes
  aglow,
And a wreath of the Christmas holly surrounding her fair
  young head,
With a circlet of glossy greenness thick set with its' berries
  red.

The sound of her "Merry Christmas!" come back through
  the vanished years,
And my heart feels a tender sorrow, my vision is dimmed
  by tears,
As I think of the voice now silent and lost to this world
  for aye,
And the fair form in earth long hidden awaiting the Judg-
  . ment Day.

The hues of the picture fade not in the sweet face and eyes
    of trust,
Though the form of *my* Christmas herald has long since
    returned to dust,
And, in place of the Christmas holly, with its green leaves
    and berries gay,
The crown of a ransomed angel on her spirit brow shines
    to-day.

Some time I shall once more see her, when my sorrows and
    cares are o'er,
And again I shall hear her greeting, on another and better
    shore ;
And the day that shall bring that meeting is one that I
    long to see,
For a last, long merry Christmas with her presence will
    come to me.

The picture brings back the shadow of the sorrow of buried
    years,
But the tenderest joys of mortals are ever akin to
    tears.
Half in joy, half in pain, I gaze on the child with her
    crown of green,
As I dream and yearn·for the meeting with my long-lost
    Holly Queen.

Camden, N. J. Dec. 4th, 1886.

SOMETIME; NOT NOW.

I can not see her, though I strain my eyes
  To pierce the shades that hid her years ago ;
The darkness and the bitter tears that rise
  Still veil the land we mortals may not know.
Gone is the face I fondly learned to love,
Forever from this world to that above.

I can not hear the tones that once were dear,
  In the glad days that never will return ;
Their echoes died away forever here,
  Leaving torn, aching hearts and eyes that burn,
Mourning a loss that earth can never fill,
And wounds time has not healed, and never will.

I know that face no more my eyes will meet ;
  Death's barriers on earth can ne'er be crossed.
I know that voice my ears can never greet,
  But even yet I can not make her lost.
I almost see her in the world of souls ;
Almost to me her whisper's echo rolls.

It can not be far to that summer land,
   When dwellers there and on this hither side
Are bound by strong ties that the years withstand,
   And thought and influence cross the parting tide.
We are not sundered wide by tomb and pall;
Death's stream is but a brooklet, after all.

They can not come to us; that bound is set.
   Our feet must cross to them in realms beyond.
One day we'll join our lost ones, but not yet!
   Greet them with words of love and glances fond.
Some day that meeting will my heart rejoice;
I'll see her face again, and hear her voice!

Long Island, Me., Feb. 3rd, 1889.

WAITING EVERMORE.

Waiting evermore, I linger
  For a step that cometh not;
Eagerly I look and listen
For the eyes with love a-glisten,
For the sweet voice of the singer
  That once blessed my earthly lot;
But in sad and silent weeping
I my lonely watch am keeping
For no presence comes to fling a
  Glory round life's darkest spot.

Those light feet, in music falling
  By my own in days of yore,
Have outstripped my own forever,
And, on earth, my ears will never
Hear again that voice enthralling;
  She has reached the farther shore.
Golden gates of death's to-morrow
Guard her from all earthly sorrow,
And my heart is vainly calling,
  Waiting, waiting evermore.

Long Island, Me., Dec. 11th, 1889.

THE NEW-MADE GRAVE.

There's a new-made mound on the bleak hillside,
   In among the graves that were there before,
And, though Fame knew not of the one that died,
   There's a spot in a few hearts aching sore;
But the living must wait, and watch, and weep,
Though the dead lie low in the last long sleep.

There's a tender face that is seen no more,
   And with anguish missed from the silent room,
And a pure soul sped to the spirit shore,
   Whose clay-cell crumbles in yonder tomb ;
But the living must sob in their sorrow sore,
While their loved sing psalms on a sunlit shore.

There's a vacant place at the board to-night,
   And an empty chair that is viewed with tears :
Glory graves no epitaph glittering bright,
   But the plain white stone is a grief for years
To those who ponder with pain and prayer
Why parting should life's chords asunder tear.

There's a break in the circle around the hearth,
  A gem, from Love's diadem lost, to mourn,
A link of its rosary reft from earth,
  A leaf from its missal is stripped and torn ;
But the living must linger, and long, and love,
Though the Lord has summoned their lost above.

There are some sad souls that are near despair,
  With an aching void there is naught can fill,
Though the proud and haughty nor think nor care
  That the humble heart has at last grown still.
Death has crushed and ruined the casket bars,
But the jewel it held is beyond the stars.

Long Island, Me., Nov. 4th, 1889.

A MEMORY PICTURE.

Out of the mighty portals of the past,
  From the dim mystery of vanished years,
In perfect beauty, too serene to last,
  This picture to my spirit's eye appears:

A vast, black, moonless, arching dome above,
  Where each great star in burning beauty glows,
The solemn stillness of a shadowed grove,
  A midnight landscape holy in repose.

A silent mansion looming dark and still,
  A pale face smiling from the open door,
Great, dark eyes shining through the tears that fill,
  Out from the shadows: this — and nothing more.

Only a sweet remembrance of the past,
  The recollection of a fond good-bye,
Whose sorrow-haunted memory will last
  Unchanged and fresh as changing moments fly.

Sometime that face will smile on me again —
  But from the open door of Paradise ;
Not from the shadows, but God's light within ;
  With joy, not tear-drops, shining in the eyes.

North Fayette, Me., Jan. 2nd, 1890.

HUMOROUS POEMS.

THE POEM MILL.

Of telephones, and phonographs, and such things I had
    read,
Until a great and dizzy thought went spinning through my
    head.
Inventors often fame achieve, and fortune, — why not I?
Glory and millions are not bad, so I was bound to try.

The papers of these latter days are slopped around with
    rhyme
That, read by chance, is apt to prove most awful half the
    time,
And so I thought I'd compass wealth and into glory jump,
And flood the world with poetry through some new patent
    pump.

And so I studied hard and long to build me a machine
To grind out better poems than the world has often seen,
Ode, sonnet, rondeau, elegy, dirge, serenade or song,
By inch or quarter, yard or mile, big, little, short or long.

Enough to say, the work was done.   A gorgeous looking
    thing,
Complete and shining everywhere in bar, and wheel, and
    spring,
Was locked into my room with me, undreamed of and
    unknown.   .
I meant to touch the critter off in silence and alone.

I knew not how the thing would work, or if 'twould work
    at all,
Or to what style the drum was set through which it was to
    squall.
I was a good deal scared, I own, but, like a little man,
I turned the valve — a whir, a squeak, and the machine
    began :

    "I loves my love and my love loves me ;
    I loves her better nor catnip tea ;
    I sticks to her like a pot o' glue,
    Cyclones can't bust our love in tew."

I didn't like that sort of thing, too soft it was by far,
And so I gave a little pull upon the tension-bar ;
At once it started off again, but took another text.
These are the grand and solemn words I heard it utter next:

    " The spangled skies in glory shine,
      As countless worlds together sing,
    And praise and melody divine
      Each night through heavens arches ring."

"A hymn of praise," I cried in joy, "what majesty of
    tone !
A mighty work have I achieved; world-wide shall I be
    known !"
But there, alas ! some jar displaced the cylinder or drum,
And in a wink the sacred style had gone to kingdom come.

    " Big feet kept time to fiddles' play,
    The 'baccy burned, rum slipped away,
    In short, the divil was to pay
    In Pat Maloney's kitchen."

Those were the words that smote my ears; I shuddered
    there in fear
Of what might be forthcoming next. Ere I could interfere,
The belt slipped half-way off the wheel; away it went
    again,
But though it never made a stop, it struck another strain :

    " On Linden, when the sun was low ;
    I saw a base-ball umpire's woe.
    So pesky loud he had to holler
    He'd split in two his paper collar."

The crazy thing was half run down, so weaker grew the
    spring ;
It jumped the track and something new it then began to
    sing,
And at the sad and tender lines all melted was my heart ;
I heaved a sigh and in my eyes the tears began to start.

" Under the daisies her form lies forever,
   Love can not clasp it low under the sod ;
But her pure soul has returned to the giver ;
   She is at rest in the bosom of God."

The tension-bar broke half in two ; I knew it had a flaw ;
Off on a tangent flew the mill ; such sense I never saw
In a thing lifeless. Though of course they'd not apply
        to me,
Yet it said things embarrassing, as you must plainly see :

" ' Rock-a-bye baby,' you rest from your cares ;
Papa hugs the nurse-girl out on the back stairs.
His moustache is tickling her little pink ear ;
Good Lord ! if the mistress that smacking should hear ! "

Though, as I said, its words to me could never be applied,
I gave a spring of lightning speed and reached that
        demon's side.
I hit the thing a furious slap and shook a pulley clear ;
I knew I would need heaven's help if my wife chanced to
        hear.

" You can't write a poem, you haven't the sense ;
Your head is a pudding, your brain is so dense !
You think you're a great one, you're only a fool ;
Get a bake on your top-piece, and go let it cool ! "

In this way it had started off, but, ere I'd time to stir,
The tension-bar broke quite apart, a snap, a crash, a whir,
And it had stopped ; and since that time it can't be made
      to go ; ·
But mighty glad of it I am, it got to talking so !

Long Island, Me., May 27th, 1889.

THE GIRL OF TO-DAY.

An Instructive Dialogue.

Tell me, what is the girl of to-day?
And what is she made of I say,
  As to what Nature lacked?
  And how does she act,
The model she-dude of to-day?

How is a girl's hair dressed to-day?
Snarled in a most horrible way,
  Then capped with a switch,
  Daubed with sugar and pitch,
Then combed in her eyes, so they say!

About the girls' faces to-day,
What is it on them, tell me, pray?
  "Lily-white" and "rose-pink,"
  And Indian ink
Or burnt cloves on their eyebrows, they say!

How is a girl's form made to-day?
And how is it fashioned, I pray?
  Of whale-bone and steel,
  Paper, cotton, rags, meal,
On a human foundation, they say!

How is a girl's foot dressed to-day?
And what is that made of, I pray?
    Of bunion and corn,
    And French heels stuck on
Shoes three sizes small, so they say!

And what does a girl wear to-day,
When she goes on her proud, mashing way?
    Dresses with monstrous trails
    To trip up the males,
And four acres of hat, so they say!

And how are their sleeves made to-day?
Tight as candle-molds every way,
    Snug as a sausage skin;
    They can only get in
By greasing their arms, so they say!

And what does a girl do to-day,
To pass the long hours, I pray?
    Read novels or flirt,
    Or sit in the dirt,
Till her mother can clear it away!

And what else can a girl do to-day?
Sit at the piano and play,
    Or squeal at a mouse,
    Or sing in the house
Till the neighbors have all moved away!

How know you the girl of to-day?
When you see a thing limping away,
　All padding and bang,
　And giggle and slang,
You may know 'tis a girl of to-day!

Port Republic, N. J., Dec. 26th, 1885.

ONCE.

There was a youth, a dashing youth,
  Whose heart was blithe and gay,
But often (if we tell the truth)
  He gazed across the way.

There was a maid, a lovely maid,
  Who with coquettish art
Upon that youth's soft feelings played,
  Until she won his heart.

There was a dad, a savage dad,
  Who kept the youth at bay,
And said for him it would be bad
  To come across the way.

There was a night, a lovely night,
  The youth could wait no more,
But sallied forth in trembling fright
  To that unfriendly door.

There was a dog, a monstrous dog,
  The dad had placed on guard.
He saw the youth's slow, cautious jog,
  And crouched down in the yard.

Once.

There was a leap, a flying leap ;
　The youth had turned to flee ;
The dog's teeth went in pretty deep
　A foot above the knee.

There was a shriek, a frenzied shriek,
　The youth he tore away ;
Swearing as fast as he could speak,
　He dashed across the way.

There were some pants, some Sunday pants,
　That once had looked so neat,
But now, through fortune's cruel chance,
　They haven't any seat.

There was a day, a mournful day,
　That youth felt rather queer,
And had to stand up any way
　With plasters in the rear.

There is a youth, a timid youth,
　Who says, with dismal groan,
His duty's plain to him, forsooth,
　To let the girls alone.

Long Island, Me., Dec. 8th, 1883.

GEESE.

A sturdy goose from the farm-yard came,
    And his post in the highway took,
And before a carriage he hissed and squalled,
   . While his huge wings he flapped and shook.
The horse, amazed at his threatening air,
    Stopped short, and the road was won ;
 But the whip's touch urged and the gander fled,
    Hissing still, as the team dashed on.

So many a man in this world of ours
    Is full of his blustering noise,
And his threatening manners will ofttimes stop
    Strong movements his squall annoys.
But those who steadily onward press,
    Find his bluster is void of use ;
In spite of flapping, and squawk, and noise,
    He is naught but a harmless goose.

North Fayette, Me., July 28th, 1889.

THE POOR POET'S PEGASUS.

My Pegasus, sure, is the queerest of creatures !
He has a horse-laugh on his asinine features,
He's lean and he's lazy, he's ragged and funny,
He's hungry and balky, and won't bring the money.

This steed of the Muse is ill-fitted for flying,
Since no one can tell for what point he is trying ;
If he don't dump one off in his crazy careering,
Like a kite with no tail, he is far beyond steering.

His thin coat is rough, and his wing lacking feathers ;
His gait is uncertain in all sorts of weathers ;
His back is too sharp to ride feeling contented ;
He kicks, bites and flounders as if half-demented.

He never can soar like an eagle, far from it !
Or blaze through the skies like a heaven-born comet ;
Ah, no ! He would miss of whatever he ran at,
Flopping off like a goose, when he's built like a gannet.

And bridled and brought upon plain terra firma,
His antics would make the most patient bard murmur.
He stumbles and bolts, and his staggers are jerky ;
He sprawls all around like a spavined hen-turkey.

He's into all fields, knocking over spectators,
With elephant feet digging all men's potatoes;
All my neighbor's fences he jumps or he grapples,
And with my head bangs off the best of their apples.

No wonder I look preternaturally solemn,
With back-bone bumped sore on his sharp spinal column
In some trip poetic, and tender with banging
My head into everything over it hanging!

Or that I feel sick, on some grand expedition
Pitched head over heels and a thing of derision,
Or when all my neighbors look madder than Persians
At damage he does on his crazy excursions!

A horse of the Muses, like that in my stable,
To prize as a gift of the gods, I'm unable!
His work is too ill-done to swap it for treasure,
And his back's too sharp to make riding a pleasure.

The cynical world doubtless dubs me "Fanatic,"
Spurring on this strange steed in a course so erratic,
When, heels over head, mud so often I land on,
Yet my horse infernal I can not abandon.

I can't pasture out the abominable creature,
For dear to my heart is each comical feature!
Though only a damage and all men deride him,
As long as I live I shall sometimes bestride him!

North Fayette, Me., Jan. 2nd, 1890.

A FOOL'S FATE.

There was a fool, a great big fool, who into trouble fell,
And every earthly reason was, he liked the girls so well;
For if he saw a pretty face, it drew him o'er the road,
As onions draw an Irishman, or beetle-bugs a toad!

Whenever he went on the street, he surely tried to flirt,
And, as a certain consequence, was always getting hurt.
A few of his adventures now I purpose to relate,
In hope of warning others ere eternally to late.

One day he went out walking in a muddy country lane;
The road was soft, the ditches full, there'd been a heavy
                rain.
He saw a pretty girl; she smiled; he blindly made a rush,
And, slipping, tumbled in the ditch and drank a quart of
                slush!

Another time, when on the street, upon the second floor
He spied a face that hit him worse than any had before.
While gazing up at her with all his eyes, and heart, and
                soul,
He walked into a coal-hole, plump upon a heap of coal!

When he got out, he looked like some coal-heaver in
       disguise;
He'd hit his head upon a brick and buttoned up his eyes,
For he went down through crosswise, a proceeding some-
       what wrong,
Scraping a peeling off his nose at least four inches long.

But, alas! he learned no wisdom from this melancholy fate,
And did the same thing once again, for, to the truth
       relate,
He three weeks afterward beheld another face above,
And once again the poor fool fell most awfully in love!

Again he walked as in a dream, not seeing where he went,
And again no guardian angel her kind, saving influence
       lent;
He stepped on a banana-skin, and on the walk beneath
He sat down with such emphasis he loosened all his teeth!

One time he saw a pretty flirt who, turning, winked her eye;
He rushed off almost crazy just to think he couldn't fly,
But he met an iron Chinaman, a horse's hitching-post,
And got his stomach butted till he 'most gave up the
       ghost!

And so his bad luck followed him, it always happened so;
He always got into a scrape each time he played the beau.
One time a girl's horse kicked him and made four bones
       in his leg,
And one girl yanked his ear until the sinner had to beg!

One angry lover batted him till he looked rather queer,
With his old proboscis canted over toward his larboard ear!
One savage father flung him through the door so mighty
        hard
That he landed in the cistern on his head, in the back
        yard!

One great big brother gave his head and heels an awful
        turn,
And, wrong end upward, used him like the dasher of a
        churn!
A raging husband chewed his ear, and then nnhung his jaw,
And in a breach-of-promise case he lost his all at law!

A would-be bridegroom kicked his shins till they were raw
        and sore;
Another took him for a mop and with him scrubbed the
        floor!
One heartless damsel stole his watch and pocket-book, and
        fled;
One scratched him till our country's flag is no more striped
        with red!

And when once more ·he got engaged, upon his wedding
        day,
With a big, one-eyed Dutchman his intended ran away!
Then he desired no more of life and so, preferring death,
He hitched a halter on a beam and yanked away his
        breath!

Now, all you fools who read this tale, mark well this fool
       of mine,
And just look out for mischief when you see a girl's eye
       shine !
So may you shun these accidents, of which the Muses sing,
And never, like him, end your life by jumping down a
       string.

Monmouth Ridge, Me., May 16th, 1884.

ADVICE TO THE BOYS.

Of all queer things on the earth below,
   Which you find as around you rove,
For foolishness nothing can stand a show
   With a fellow that's dead in love.

He sighs like the bellows of a blacksmith's shop,
   He stands and stares at the moon ;
He talks of his dear like he never would stop,
   And he acts like a crazy old loon.

He never has a thought of the cares of life,
   And hash never enters his mind,
For he thinks, if only he captures a wife,
   They can both of them live on wind. .

In short, he acts like a double-dyed fool,
   A natural, who doesn't know beans,
And is soft as mush till his head gets cool,
   Or he finds what a family means.

But don't make fun of the fellows in love,
   For maidens all hearts will steal,
And you never will know, till your own shall move,
   How very like fools they feel.

So let them be soft as a well-cooked squash,
  Or the dough on the pantry shelf,
For ten to one, when you're some girl's mash,
  You will be just as bad yourself.

Long Island, Me., Dec. 9th, 1886.

THE MEASURE OF ALL THINGS.

Wise and wicked the world is growing,
   The honest and simple go to the wall;
None care how a man's life is going,
   If he's successful, why, that is all.
Guilt as black as the source of evil
   Counts for a naught in these latter days;
None ask if you are saint or devil,
   When your efforts success repays.

Raise yourself, kick over your neighbor,
   You can climb up by those knocked down;
If you win through the meanest labor,
   You are the best man about the town.
Right and wrong are fast changing places;
   The greatest evil is being poor,
Truth and poverty are disgraces;
   Guilt successful is goodness, sure!

Get you money and get you honor,
   Beg them, steal them, no matter how.
If you miss them, you are a goner;
   If you gain them, all heads will bow.

People judge you by your achieving,
  Not the way that the thing is gained ;
Do it by lying, cheating and thieving,
  No matter how, if the end's attained !

Get you riches and win successes ;
  Crimes successful to honors grow !
Smash the decalogue all to pieces,
  Poverty is the worst vice, you know.
Stay at the bottom, and you are a sinner,
  Rise by any means, you are a saint ;
Number One care for ; if you are the winner,
  Of your record there's no complaint !

You are good as you meet successes,
  And if fortune your steps attend,
You are prized, and will meet caresses,
  If you always attain your end.
Only one thing makes good or evil ;
  By it men judge beyond redress,
Send you to heaven or to the devil ;
  The measure of all things is success !

Port Republic, N. J., March 24th, 1886.

KISSING IN THE DARK.

My heart is sad and heavy,
  My trials sore oppress ;
Perhaps I should feel better,
  If I should just confess !

I have severely suffered,
  As you at once will find,
Soon as I come to tell you
  What weighs upon my mind.

You must know I am bashful,
  And don't know how to spark,
And what caused all my trouble
  Was kissing in the dark.

I never had been courting,
  But last night thought I'd start,
And call upon a lady
  Whose beauty broke my heart.

No·wonder it felt shaky
  The damsel's house before,
And flew round like a button
  Upon a cellar door !

My face shone like a sunset,
　And fairly scorched my hair !
I wished, when she was coming,
　I might die then and there.

She asked me to the parlor,
　And we were all alone.
After a little season
　I had some bolder grown.

At last I got quite near her,
　Though scared beyond a doubt.
Somehow — I can't explain it —
　The parlor lamp went out.

My courage then rose higher,
　And, filled with lover's bliss,
I had the cheek to ask her
　If I might have a kiss.

At first she told me, "No, Sir !"
　But soon she said I might ;
If then she could have seen me
　I should have died of fright !

I stopped a while in terror,
　Then thought I'd better try
And kiss her in the darkness ; —
　I hit her in the eye !

That made me somewhat flustered,
  As you may well suppose,
And so, when next I tried it,
  I bit her on the nose.

Then I became more flurried,
  But once more waded in ;
This time I fared no better,
  I only lapped her chin.

Then in my desperation,
  About half dead with fear,
I made another trial,
  And slobbered in her ear.

When next I tried it, judging
  From the way my nose feels,
I must have gone about it
  Like someone spearing eels.

So hard it punched her forehead
  That still it sidewise hangs,
And all the effort gained me
  Was just a chew of bangs.

The last time I attempted,
  I didn't hit at all,
But smacked her father's picture
  Hung on the parlor wall.

Kissing in the Dark.

In agony of terror,
  I bolted out of that;
I never stopped for manners,
  Or even for my hat!

The sore nose and the frighting
  Of that experience,
I feel quite sure, have taught me
  A little common-sense!

And if, a thing most doubtful,
  Again I try to spark,
I never will be guilty
  Of kissing in the dark!

Port Republic, N. J., Feb. 9th, 1886.

A COURTING EXPERIENCE.

Jane Jones was acknowledged the Boobytown belle,
　　And by her great beauty was known ;
She'd a form like a scarecrow, as many could tell,
　　And feet hippopotamus grown.

She'd a nose like a coffee-pot after a ride
　　Of a mile at the tail of a dog,
A mouth where old Mammoth Cave surely could hide,
　　And teeth like burnt stumps in a bog.

Sam Stubbs was a youth who was crushed by her charms,
　　And he, too, was handsome withal,
But his hair was so red when he passed by the farms
　　In the night, all the roosters would squall.

He'd a wart on his nose and a mole on his chin,
　　And a spavin he had on each knee.
He walked like a cripple encumbered with gin,
　　And he'd eyes like a " Heathen Chinee.''

Old Jones was a monster with heart like a flint,
　　And, when he discovered the mash,
He looked at poor Sam with a horrible squint,
　　'That stove his bright hopes into smash.

He told him to never come into his house,
   And to the fair Jane not to speak ;
If he did he would crack him as he would a louse,
   And kick him half-way through next week.

But Jane told poor Sammy she'd ever be true,
   And asked him to come Sunday night.
Her dad went to bed soon as daylight was through ;
   When safe she would blow out the light.

The time came, the darkness was dreadful and black ;
   The old man went early to bed,
With salve on his corns, mustard paste on his back,
   And snored fit to waken the dead.

Jane blew out the lamp, Sam the signal obeyed,
   And started at two-forty gait ;
The wart on his nose flopped with each step he made ;
   His hair glowed like comet of fate.

He entered the house, kissed her mouth full of snags,
   As he took the fair Jane on his knees ;
Her breath floated round like the smell of old rags,
   Or the odor of Limberger cheese.

Alas, for his joy !   In the midst of his bliss,
   That wart took poor Jane in the eye,
As Sam struggled hard for another sweet kiss,
   And she squealed out a small, squeaky cry.

Her dad woke in terror, and, scared at the blaze
    That shone from Sam's fiery hair,
He sprang up and dressed in the direst amaze
    For he thought he saw flames in the air.

He rushed for the kitchen, and Sam turned to run,
    But, just as he plunged through the door,
Old Jones saw the trouble and kicked him like fun
    With the toe of his big twenty-four!

Sam rose like a comet, some ten feet or less,
    And fell with a thundering crash;
He struck on some pickets, how hard you can guess,
    For he stove the fence all into smash.

He whirled in the air like a skilled acrobat,
    Ere striking the pickets beneath;
He rose with spine punched through the crown of his hat,
    And the door-yard was all full of teeth!

He sped from the spot with all speed that he had,
    But his gait it was halting and jerky.
That wart hung straight downward, dejected and sad,
    And he limped like a setting hen-turkey.

As he passed o'er the hilltop, the sky seemed to glow
    Like a sunset, reflecting his hair.
Even now, as he tells the sad tale of his woe,
    No wonder he wishes to swear.

The dose was sufficient ; no more suitors came,
  Sam was so unfortunate there.
He walks with two canes to this day, he's so lame,
  And he hasn't a tooth he can spare.

Monmouth Ridge, Me., May 15th, 1884.

A PROBLEM.

I had a dream quite funny,
    One night when work was done;
I thought a man was asking
    Advice about his son.

I dreamed he walked the village,
    And said in eager fret,
" What shall I do with Willie?"
    To all the girls he met.

The organist he questioned,
    She gave him this reply:
" I'd use him for a scarecrow;
    The birds would surely fly."

The fair, coquettish widow,
    In her becoming crape,
Said, " Put him in the circus
    In place of Barnum's ape."

The milliner's clerk answered,
    Hearing his question faint,
" He is so green, I'd grind him
    And make him into paint."

The young post-mistress told him,
  (For still the vision ran on,)
" The boy's so awful brassy,
  I'd cast him into cannon.''

The school-ma'am quickly answered,
  With looks of eager hope,
" He is as soft as tallow ;
  I'd stir him into soap.''

My room door loudly slamming
  Soon ended all this fret,
So what to do with Willie
  Is undecided yet.

But all you other Willies,,
  Of every age and name,
Who think you're lady-killers,
  Are rated just the same !

So when the girls you're chasing,
  And acting out the fop,
Think what they said of this one,
  And you'll conclude to stop.

North Fayette, Me., March 9th, 1887.

AFTER THE CHURCH FAIR.

Jim Jones went home with Polly Ann Mower,
  And I tell you he felt nice,
When he elbowed her out of the meeting-house door,
  But he never once thought of the ice.

Yet the street was full of water and slop.
  That had frozen up during the day,
But the night was dark, and it didn't show up
  As they started on their homeward way.

Jim was whispering something tender and low,
  And Polly was smiling and sweet,
So they never once looked where they had to go
  Down the icy, slippery street.

Soon they struck a spot all glassy and smooth,
  And their feet they couldn't steer,
And down on his head came the gay, happy youth,
  While Polly sat down on his ear.

Jim's number tens kicked at the planet Mars,
  And Polly's sailed everywhere,
And the place was hid from the light of the stars
  By the feet floating round in the air.

They both crawled off from the ice on their knees,
  And sorrowfully limped away,
But many a groan floated off on the breeze,
  For they didn't feel half so gay.

The next day a traveler found the spot
  Strewn with fragments and pools of gore ;
It looked like the place a battle was fought,
  Or the wreck of a dry goods store.

When Polly went down like a mountain pine
  On the head of the youth beneath,
She did it so hard she shortened her spine,
  And jarred out half of her teeth.

Poor Jim had hit on the back of his head,
  While Polly's weight smashed his nose
And skinned four inches of it — oh, how it bled !
  And he split his new pair of — clothes !

The match is off since that dismal wreck ;
  Jim don't court Polly nowadays ?
She doesn't want a beau that will break her neck,
  He a girl that sits on his face !

Port Republic, N. J., Feb. 9th, 1886.

MEN AND PLACES.

This world is a case full of holes of all sizes
    And shapes, big and little, round, three-cornered, square,
And men are shaped likewise ; so trouble arises
    When one strikes a hole he don't fit to a hair.

Yet people are always mistaking their places,
    Mistaking their callings, their powers, their souls ;
And much of the wrong that our planet disgraces
    Is caused by men getting in ill-fitting holes.

Ofttimes a man's mind flies a decade before him,
    And grasps a great truth and proclaims it to all,
But meets hate and scorn ; e'en his friends try to floor him,
    He's a man in a hole many sizes too small.

Many simple old souls find the world rather tricky,
    And by their own honesty go to the wall.
Their angles keep catching, they find life's road sticky,
    Because they're square men in round holes, that is all.

Some others are soapy and have no opinions,
    Say, "yes, yes," to all and, "amen," to the whole,
But people despise the poor, sycophant minions ;
    Such a one's a round man in a three-cornered hole.

Sometimes paltry men are exalted to power
    And raised to positions they never could fill,
They soon are the scorn and contempt of the hour ;
    Little men in big holes never fiil up the bill.

A good farmer often becomes a poor preacher,
    A good smith turns into a law-spouting ape,
A good workman spoils changing into a teacher ;
    All are stuck into holes that are not the right shape.

There's a hole that will fit e'en the oddest-shaped human,
    There a man that will fill every hole in the case,
(Though now a great many are needing a new man ;)
    So each should be careful to find the right place.

Young men, ponder well ere you choose occupations ;
    Finding places in life will require much wit.
Endeavor to reach your appropriate stations,
    And try and get into the holes that you fit.

Port Republic, N. J., March 1st, 1886.

FLOWER SONGS.

PYXIE.

There's a fresh and a sweet tradition of the birth of the
    fairy flower
That comes in the early spring-time to bloom in the leaf-
    less bower,
And opens its star-like blossoms with a promise of brighter
    skies,
To come with the nearing summer, in its myriad upturned
    eyes.

When I gaze on the tiny tokens of a softened and buried
    woe,
My fancy flies with the legend to the dim of the long ago,
And my senses drink of a sweetness, a sadness that's not
    of earth,
As my mind goes in dream or vision to the morn of the
    floweret's birth.

A dell bathed in silver brightness of moonlight appears to
    me,
The dim, cool shadows surrounding cast by bordering
    shrub and tree ;
I hear on the passing zephyrs a melody sad arise,
Soft, plaintive, melting and tender, and low as a wild
    reed's sighs.

And, lo! in the fair, pale moonlight, in the heart of the
    inmost dell,
On a bier made of tiny flowers, where the whitest of
    moonbeams dwell,   .
Lies a motionless, lifeless figure as pale as the lilies fair,
And spotless as pure white snowflakes that float on the
    winter air.

White-robed on her flowery pillow, asleep in her final sleep,
Is the form of a fallen fairy, and round it her sisters weep;
A circle of lovely figures in gauziest whiteness dressed,
Pure, beauteous, though far too tiny to gaze o'er a linnet's
    crest.

Though low as the grasses' murmur, in my vision there
    comes to me
The soft and the wondrous sweetness of their wild, sad
    melody,
And it seems like a song from heaven, their requiem o'er
    the dead,
Though mortal ears comprehend not the words by the
    fairies said.

The low, sad chant of the mourners in cadences dies away,
And the fay and her bier of flowers sink into the earth for
    aye,
The fairy sisterhoods vanish; skies glow with the coming
    sun;
The moonlight fades from the grasses, and the funeral rites
    are done.

The rays of the early morning dart in through the twilight
    gloom
And glitter upon the dew-drops that lie on the fairy's tomb,
And where'er a fairy's tear-drop has fallen around the bier,
The blossoms of star-eyed pyxie in beauty serene appear.

And whene'er the sweet white flowers in spring-time awake
    again,
I think of the drops of anguish that gave the pure buds to
    men.
I love the sweet pyxie-blossoms and long for them to
    appear,
Yet I see in each starry flower a sorrowing fairy's tear.

North Fayette, Me., Apr. 25th, 1887.

DAISIES.

The daisies are white on the hillside,
　They float on the waves of the grass,
The foam on those billows of verdure
　That swell as the scented winds pass.
They are touched by the light, unseen fingers
　Of the breezes in loving caress,
And their eyes, pure and tender, look upward
　To Heaven's blue o'erarching to bless.

They rocked on the waves of the grasses,
　As they float on their billows to-day,
In the days of a long-vanished summer,
　Departed forever and aye ;
They nodded the same on the hillside,
　And thankfully bowed to the skies,
Whence the sunlight and shower descended
　To gladden their innocent eyes.

But the flowers of my life, then in blossom,
   With the summers come never again,
They withered and faded forever,
   Though the field-daisies blossom as then.
That summer I looked on them gladly,
   But sadly I view them to-day ;
Earth's flowers are renewed in their season,
   Life's, once gone, have vanished for aye.

West Mt. Vernon, Me., July 14th, 1886.

WILD ROSES.

Wild roses bloom by the brooklet's side,
  Where it sleeps in a deep, dark pool,
And the waving trees of the forest hide
  Fresh moss in their shadows cool.
They star the billowy banks of green,
  Each nodding its calyx bright,
As the wandering breezes glide in between
  Caressing with touch so light.

No gaudy flower from a florist's stand,
  No pampered and scentless thing,
But a blossom fresh as from God's own hand,
  Drinking deep from the crystal spring,
With a heart like the heart of a shell of pearl
  Down under the cool, green sea,
As bright as the cheek of a blushing girl
  In her maidenly modesty.

But rude hands, touching the slender stem,
   May scatter the leaves it bore,
And the fair flower, pure as a priceless gem,
   Lie shattered forevermore.
Yet the careless hand and the selfish soul
   Spoil the blossoms of light and joy;
And, alas! wild roses are not the whole
   That a rude touch can destroy.

North Fayette, Me., Aug. 13th, 1888.

MAY-FLOWERS.

There's a faint yet sweet perfume that floats in the air
   On the cold, chilling breezes of earliest May,
Ere the warm zephyrs call Summer's flowerets fair .
   From out the dark earth to adorn her bright way.

But search for the source of that odor so sweet
   At a short distance from you, and naught can you find,
But 'mid the sere grasses and leaves at your feet
   Bloom the sweet flowers unnoticed that freshen the wind.

Beneath the dead leaves of a Summer that's past,
   On the cold earth just waking from Winter's long sleep,
Under rubbish heaped on them by each chilling blast,
   The modest green leaves of the May-flower creep.

And close underneath them, concealed from the eye
   Of the careless observer, are odorous cells,
That yield their sweet fragrance as hidden they lie,
   In lovely pink clusters, the May-flower bells.

Thus oft in life's journey an influence sweet,
   Perfuming the cold, barren desert of earth,
Floats around us from buds lying close at our feet,
   While we look far away for the blossom of worth.

Beneath the sere leaves, the dead hopes of the past,
  In the desert of life all unnoticed oft lie,
Under wrecks scattered by disappointment's wild blast,
  The sweet human May-flowers so blindly passed by.

Their modest air hides the sweet blossoms of deeds,
  And so we pass by them with never a thought,
Seeking flowerets where clusters of ill-smelling weeds
  By their rank, leafy stalks our attention have caught.

Let us search out the sweet buds that bloom in our way,
  And pluck them in love on our bosoms to shine,
And cherish them fondly as long as we may.
  God bless human May-flowers, and those on the vine !

Fayette, Me., May 18th, 1885.

BUTTERCUPS.

The buttercups nodded in sunshine,
As their buds to the light unrolled ;
The wandering breezes kissed them
On their trembling crowns of gold ;
The green leaves rustled above them
And dappled the grass with shade,
On that day of a vanished summer,
As with them a fair child played.

The buttercups nod in the sunshine
The same as a year ago ;
They have slept through the long, cold winter,
To wake when the soft winds blow ;
Birds sing and leaves shake above them,
And the green earth where they wave,
But their playmate will never waken ;
They bloom on the fair child's grave.

Gordon Hill, Me., June 10th, 1886.

Scriptural & Religious Poems

BARTIMEUS.

In the days now gone forever,
In the land the Saviour walked in,
Dawned a day still unforgotten,
Dawned in beauty o'er a landscape
Fairer than a poet's fancies,
Fairer than an artist's dreamings,
Dawned to show a deed of mercy
That should fill the world with wonder.

Jericho, the mighty city,
Sat arrayed in all her beauty,
Bathed in floods of glowing sunlight,
Flinging back the day-god's splendor
In a thousand bright reflections
From her turrets, domes and towers,
Burnished by the summer sunshine,
'Till they seemed of gold the purest.

Round about that teeming city,
Like the setting of a jewel,
Lay the green fields, fair and fertile,
Covered with the waving grasses
Intermixed with fairer flowers,
That filled all the air with fragrance,
And from many a wayside shade-tree
Happy birds their songs were pouring.

Sadly by the busy roadside,
Just without the city gateway,
'Mid that scene of light and beauty,
With his head bowed in dejection,
With his beard unkempt and streaming
Wild upon the summer breezes,
Asking alms of all who passed him,
Sat the beggar, blind Bartimeus.

Naught to him were all the beauties
Lavished on that lovely landscape;
Never had his eyes beheld them;
And the happy birds above him
Seemed to mock his situation,
Mock the homeless, friendless beggar,
With his poverty to mock him,
As he sat there all unnoticed.

Suddenly from out the city,
Crowding through the open gateway,
Down the highway broad and sunny,
Came an eager throng of people,
But not one the beggar noticed ;
Not a coin bestowed upon him
Cheered the suffering and sightless,
Cheered the heart of blind Bartimeus.

There he sat with grey hair streaming,
Wild, and matted, and neglected,
With his torn and tattered garments
Scarcely shielding from the sunlight,
With his form by hunger wasted,
Piteously his sightless eyeballs
Turning as he asked assistance.

Heeding not, they still were passing,
And he turned away despairing ;
His heart filled with bitter sadness,
And the scalding tears descended
As he felt himself unnoticed
And his sorest needs neglected ;
But a sudden hope thrilled through him,
As he heard the Master's accents.

Then his voice he straightway lifted,
Crying out amid the clamor
Of the rabble all unheeding,
Crying out in wild entreaty,
As the throng still hurried forward,
Crying out in tones beseeching
The one anguished supplication,
" Jesus, Lord, have mercy on me ! "

" Hold thy peace ! " the people answered,
Viewing him with looks disdainful,
As they scornfully passed by him,
But the more his voice he lifted ;
Louder grew the tones entreating,
And above the noise and tumult
The wild prayer came to the Master,
" Jesus, Lord, have mercy on me ! "

Then in pity turned the Saviour,
With a smile of heavenly beauty
On His face of loving mildness,
Saying to the crowd that followed
Closely on His steps departing
From the lovely eastern city,
For His heart o'erflowed with mercy
For the beggar, " Bring him hither ! "

Flinging down his tattered garment,
Straightway rose up blind Bartimeus,
And with eager footsteps hastened,
Through the throng that now divided,
To where still the Master waited ;
And with hope and fear commingled,
In his heart a prayer unspoken,
Tremblingly he stood before Him.

Then the saintly Man of Sorrows
Smiled again upon the beggar,
Knowing all his great desire,
All his fear and all his trembling,
Knowing all the faith within him,
Spoke again in mildest accents,
As the blind man bowed before Him,
Saying unto him, "What would'st thou?"

Eagerly Bartimeus answered,
Half in hope and half in fearing,
Hoping his wish might be granted,
Fearing bitter disappointment,
Answered without stop or staying,
Answered trembling with excitement,
All his eager soul outpouring,
"Lord, that I might have my eyesight!"

To the Master's brow compassion
Added yet another beauty,
And his sinless face grew brighter
With the glowing look of mercy,
And in tones of love and pity,
The Great Teacher, pure and holy,
Spoke the words of blesséd import,
"Go thy way, thy faith hath healed thee."

Like a flash the eyes were opened
That had never seen the sunlight,
And the scene of summer splendor
Dawned on the awakened vision
Of a mind that had in darkness
Lived until that present moment,
Like a new-created Eden,
Or a blesséd dream of Heaven.

Then he saw the city glowing
In the streaming summer sunshine,
Saw the green fields decked with flowers,
Saw the dark and distant hill-tops,
The o'er-arching blue of Heaven,
Saw the throng around him standing,
And amid that scene of beauty
Christ's face beaming like an angel's.

Fairer than his fairest dreamings,
Nature's works around were scattered ;
Lovelier than aught e'er imagined.
Jericho loomed up behind him ;
And deep gratitude o'ercame him,
And love for the Great Physician,
Who had raised the cloud of darkness
That from him had hidden all things.

No more seemed the birds to mock him
With his wretched life of sorrow,
With his gloomy, dark existence,
But in joy they sang above him ;
And no more the world seemed to him
Cold and cheerless and despairing,
But a Paradise of beauty
Fitted for the angels' dwelling.

Out from Jericho the Master
Went His way, the crowd attending,
Through the scene of summer beauty,
'Mid the songs of countless birdlings ;
And behind in fond devotion,
Gratitude and love unbounded,
Praising God for all His blessings,
Went Bartimeus, blind no longer.

Fayette, Me., June 10th, 1885.

NOW I LAY ME.

"Now I lay me down to sleep;
  I pray the Lord my soul to keep.
If I should die before I wake,
  I pray the Lord my soul to take."

My mother taught me at her knee
  Those childlike words of purity,
And bade me breathe to One above
  That prayer for His protecting love.

Borne backward by the dear old rhyme,
  My mind flies to the happy time
When my young life was fresh and fair,
  Unshadowed by sin, pain, or care.

From out the portals of the past
  Fond memories come crowding fast,
And visions bright I seem to see,
  Of what was, but no more shall be.

Again I see my mother's face,
  And feel her loving arm's embrace,
As when, long since, beside her seat
  I learned those lines so old and sweet.

But childhood's time has passed for aye ;
　'Tis years since thus I learned to pray,
And all the winding ways I've trod
　Have lead me farther from my God.

Oh ! for the childish lips of truth,
　That framed those words in sinless youth,
As, kneeling by my mother's chair,
　I learned that well-remembered prayer !

My feet have turned so far away,
　He scarce can hear me when I pray,
Yet, though sin's waves above me break,
　"I pray the Lord my soul to take !"

Melrose, Mass., Oct. 21st, 1887.

THE TEMPEST.

Night wrapped the sea's broad bosom.   Darkness deep
Hung heavily around.   No golden star
Pierced with its cheering ray the inky air.
Over the billows swept the roaring gale
And lashed them into fury; high they leaped,
Assaulting heaven in impious impotence,
Flinging their white spume through the murky skies,
And then in sullen anger falling back
Upon the waves behind them.

             Death was there,
With all his terrors; through the howling night
He cleft the darkness of the raging storm
With tireless pinion, gloating o'er a ship
That struggled with the waters and the gale,
As if she knew the precious freight she bore.

Fiercer the storm-wind fought her; higher yet
The billows rose around her; lower still
She settled in the water, deeply filled
By great waves breaking o'er her; darker yet
The night became; and fainter yet the hope
Of the worn, toiling crew, who seemed to hear
A death-song mingling with the screaming gale.

Through the wild night a wailing, anguished plaint
Rang as the frightened sailors felt the end
Of all things earthly drawing on apace,
At least for them. From their faint, failing hearts,
In wild beseeching, came the pleading cry,
"Master, we perish here; carest thou not?"
Then the calm Sleeper woke from quiet sleep,
And calmly round on the wild scene He gazed,
The terror-stricken men, the raging sea,
Then to the storm said calmly, "Peace; be still!"

The loud waves heard that voice and sank to rest;
The wild winds heard it, murmured and grew still;
Death heard, and spread his dusky wings in flight;
The clouds divided; sweetly shone the stars
On the sea's breast, reflecting those above;
And there *was* peace; no strife, no doubt, no fear,
But on the quiet scene there reigned a night
As still, as fair, as peaceful as the eves
That smiled in Eden ere the fall of man :
There was a calm.

West Mt. Vernon, Me., July 16th, 1886.

THE PRODIGAL'S PRAYER.

Wandering far from the home of my youth,
With naught my own but my sorrow and ruth,
Still my heart cries out wherever I roam ;
Father, oh, Father ! once more take me home !

Far have I wandered from right's narrow track,
Almost too far for me e'er to go back,
Yet thou dost love me wherever I roam ;
Father, oh, Father ! once more take me home !

Nothing I bring from the world and its strife,
Nothing I have but the wreck of my life.
Let me return to youth's home as of yore ;
Father, oh, Father ! receive me once more !

Sin is around, and its stains are on me,
Naught that is good in my life can I see.
Out of the depths do I cry in my pain ;
Oh, Father, take me ! Receive me again !

All the enticements that lured me away,
Proved hollow snares that could only betray,
False beacons set on life's storm-beaten shore ;
From the wreck, Father, receive me once more !

Oh, how I long for the blessings I spurned,
Ere to the world and its vices I turned!
Is it too late? In sin still must I roam?
Father, oh, Father! I pray take me home!

In all my sin and my vileness I call;
Give me the home that was mine ere my fall!
The wretched prodigal calls from the wild;
Take home, oh, Father! thy wandering child!

Port Republic, N. J., Feb. 2nd, 1886.

A LEGEND.

There's a beautiful legend of days long ago,
  When Christ dwelt on earth among men,
That he walked with the twelve·He had chosen below
  To tell His glad message again ;
And they saw by the roadside a sickening sight,
  A putrid dog's mouldering form,
Decaying and festering in the sun's light
  Which fell there serenely and warm.

The Master's disciples passed by in disgust
  At the animal's foulest decay,
And only came near for the reason they must
  In order to pass on their way ;
And they said, each to each, as they gazed on the dead,
  " What a foul and horrible sight ! "
The Lord smiled upon them in kindness and said,
  " Yet his teeth are a beautiful white."

So is it in life in the darkest of scenes,
    In sickness, vice, crime and despair ;
'Twixt foulest corruptions some good intervenes.
    There is something fair everywhere.
In the vilest of hearts that sin's shadow enfolds
    And renders as black as the night,
The Lord, overlooking in mercy, beholds
    Something still a pure, beautiful white.

Port Republic, N. J., Oct. 25th, 1885.

O, FATHER, HEAR ME!

O, Father, hear me though my sins are many,
  For Thou canst cleanse and take them all away!
Though small indeed my worth, if I have any,
    Help me, I pray!

Keep me from evils 'mid the world's temptation,
  I would do well, but oh! the flesh is weak.
Accept my spirit's humble consecration;
    For Thee I seek.

The way is dark, my Father, oh! protect me;
  Shield me from harm by Thine unfailing care.
When life is over, oh! do Thou elect me
    Thy love to share.

Hold Thou my hand, whatever be the morrow;
  Lead me through this life to the one to be;
Be with me still, in pleasure or in sorrow
    Abide with me.

Grant Thou that I may bring, ere life be ended,
  Some golden grain amid the thorns and tares,
Some few good deeds with sin's dark actions blended;—
    Oh, hear my prayers!

Guide Thou my way amid the gathering shadows ;
  Lead Thou me on from darkness into light,
From sin's dark fields to fair, Elysian meadows
      Forever bright.

Oh ! grant that, when I pass the shades surrounding
  That long have wrapped my way in gloomy night,
My soul may share Thy tenderness abounding
      In worlds of light !

Lord, at the last let all my guilt of sinning
  Fall from me like a mantle cast aside :
And may my soul, pure as at life's beginning,
      With Thee abide.

Long Island, Me., Jan 5th, 1888.

SAMSON'S SOLILOQUY.

Here lean I, wearied, on the massive shafts,
Whose mighty limbs once never knew fatigue,
The sport of the loud rabble gathered round
The captive giant, feeble, blinded, shorn,
Enslaved, a thing for taunts and mockery.

Once these strong arms in slaughter never tired,
Though hundreds sank in death beneath their strokes ;
Once thoughts rushed seething through this subtle brain,
And tricks and stratagems destroyed my foes ;
Once I was loved by God and feared by man ;
And now, behold me here, a massive wreck,
A slave among the vilest, loathed, abhorred,
Spit on and smitten by the hand of man,
And stricken by the Lord whom I forsook,
As now in wrath He has forsaken me !

How have I fallen from my high estate,
To be the jest of fools !   Oh, bitter thought !
I only am the source of all my woes,
The maker of my fate ! To basest use
I put the powers lent me from above,
And so I lost them ! Leaving the Most High,
I turned aside unto a godless tribe,
And cast off all things that I once held dear,
Lured by the falseness of an angel face.

Swift came the retribution ; mocked, betrayed,
Sold into bondage by a traitor kiss
From her I loved, for whom I sacrificed
Friends, home and country, character and God,
And brought so low none see me but to scorn ;
E'en to myself a loathing and contempt !

O, fool ! fool ! fool ! to trust an impious race !
O worse than fool to trust a woman's smile,
When I had cause to doubt ! A woman's heart
Will shame a devil by its wickedness,
If she be evil ! Man ne'er sinks so low
As fallen woman ; depths on depths divide
The sundered pair, though both be steeped in sin.
Her soul has powers and capabilities
For good or evil his can ne'er attain,
Wielding an influence not to be withstood ;
An angel or a fiend ; from Adam down,
A woman was lead on to weal or woe !

O, fairest face on earth ! O, foulest heart,
To bring a faithful, loving life to this !
Well am I punished. May the Lord forgive,
As sometimes I dare dream He can and will,
When sudden thrills dart through my weakened form
As if the harbingers of coming strength,
Like that of days gone by ! So may it be !
Just is my fate ; nor murmur nor complaint
Should pass my lips ; but, oh ! 'tis very hard !

Would that my former powers might be restored
To cause the hooting multitude around
To fear the enemy they curse and mock,
And teach them to respect! Gladly would I
Myself destroy to crush my scornful foes.

Lord, for this once my vanished strength restore,
Till I these massive pillars wrench away,
And hurl the roof in ruin on the throng,
One last, fell blow destroying them and me.
Ha! It comes back! They tremble in my grasp!
I feel them totter! O, I thank Thee, Lord!
One effort more; the tense cords strain and part
But the stones grate again; the pillars sway,
They break! They fall! The mighty stones above
Rush headlong from on high! Revenge and death! —

Long Island, Me., Jan. 1st, 1889.

HOPES AND DREAMS.

Dreams of my boyhood allured, then bereft me,
  Hopes for the future born only to fade;
Wiser perhaps, surely sadder, they left me
  By graves where fancy's bright children are laid.

Things are, alas! far from what I once deemed them,
  In the old days when my glad life was new;
Could they be what then so fondly I dreamed them,
  Scarce would I care heaven's gate to go through.

Bright were the visions encircling my slumbers,
  Gorgeous the day-dreams that gladdened my heart;
Now bitter truth my sad spirit encumbers,
  From fancies fond sternly bidding me part.

Evermore gone are those splendors ideal,
  Ne'er to come back till time ceases for me.
Face to face now with the cruelly real,
  Passed through the rainbows, clouds only I see.

Yet I thank God for those hopes from me taken;
  Better illusion gild sorrow's dark pall,
Better from bright dreams in pain to awaken
  Than have real gloom hanging heavy on all.

Long Island, Me., Jan. 23d, 1889.

NOTHING BUT LEAVES.

I'm nearing the future that's rising before me,
   Approaching the goal to which all journeys run ;
I'm leaving the clouds that were just bending o'er me ;
   I'm nearing death's valley — and what have I done?

Other people around me are happy in labor,
   And they would be missed should they happen to die ;
They, and their work too, are a joy to their neighbor,
   And helps to the whole world—but what good am I?

The great earth has work for the pure and true-hearted,
   There's need for the thinkers and doers to be ;
They're missed and lamented when they have departed,
   They're wanted,—but what is there needful in me?

Who cares if to-morrow the grave shall enfold me ?
   What good have I yet done by deed or by thought?
What tie have I made that to this life should hold me ?
   My life, and my work, and myself, all are naught.

Why still stands the tree that the garden encumbers,
   The stalk that has borne neither blossom nor fruit?
I've nothing but leaves ! Let me go to my slumbers,
   Unmissed, for, judged by my past life, I am mute.

Port Republic, N. J., March 16th, 1886.

THE PRODIGAL'S RETURN.

Mother, I come
Back from life's war, crushed by scorn and defeat ;
Wounded and broken, to lie at your feet,
Conquered, I come.

Yes, I come back,
Back to the shelter I knew as a boy,
Whence I rushed into the world in my joy ;—
Wearily back.

Coming once more,—
For hope's bright day-star before me has paled,
Sadly I feel I have fought and have failed,—
To childhood's door.

Gone ; all, all gone
Are the bright dreams that once dazzled my view ;
Not a trace left of the visions youth knew ;—
Faded and gone.

While pulses beat,
Never shall I know a tithe that I dreamed ;
Things are unlike what to fancy they seemed ;
Bitter defeat !

What have I won?
Crushed and flung out of the world's busy track,
Hopes of my childhood will never come back;
    Blasted each one!

Bearing in vain,
Back to the home that once proudly I spurned,
From the world's glare that allured and then burned,
    Ashes and pain!

Coming from sin,
Not as I left in my strength and my prime,
But a wreck tossed from the billows of time,
    A " might have been ! "

Take me once more,
Mother; my strivings for glory are done,
My deeds unwrought and my laurels unwon,
    Lost evermore!

Long Island, Me., Feb. 11th, 1837.

"WHATEVER COMETH, COMETH WELL."

Over me now the future hangs impending,
　What it may hold no mortal tongue can tell;
Yet, whether far or near may be life's ending,
　I feel whatever cometh, cometh well.

I can not see the way that lies before me;
　I know not where fate may my steps impel,
Or whether light or dark skies will be o'er me,
　But yet I know what cometh, cometh well.

Pleasures may come, they will; all mortals find them;
　Sorrows may come, they must; for all they swell,
Yet something better always lies behind them;
　Pain, joy, whichever cometh, cometh well.

Our pleasures are the brightest gifts of heaven,
　Bestowed on us while here on earth we dwell;
Our sorrows are in love and mercy given,
　And for the best.　What cometh, cometh well.

Trials are to the soul like fires refining,
　Purging the gold of dross with potent spell;
So, whether cloudy be life's skies, or shining,
　The thing that cometh, surely cometh well.

I would not know what coming years are hiding;
  'Tis best that no one can the future tell.
I wait the time to be with trust confiding,
  Because whatever cometh, cometh well.

'Tis certain lights and shadows will be blended ;
  . In perfect peace no one may hope to dwell ;
But nothing will I fear till life be ended ;
  I know whatever cometh, cometh well.

I'll welcome pleasures when God's love shall grant them,
  I will submit when sorrows round me swell ;
In joy or pain I'll raise the cheering anthem,
  "Whatever cometh, surely cometh well."

Port Republic, N. J., Feb. 21st, 1886.

PRAISE SONG.

Praise God for my little, since little have I
That shows to the proud world that passes me by;
Yet blessings are lurking in trouble disguised,
And some in all life-paths should highly be prized.
Few favors of fortune may fall upon mine,
But praise God for those marks of mercy divine.

Praise God for the cottage that shelters me warm,
While others are out in the pitiless storm;
Praise Him for the true hearts returning my love,
While friendless and loveless so many must rove;
Praise Him for a home under Wisdom's control,
And not where gross ignorance shadows the soul.

Praise God for the health he has given to me,
While sick and afflicted about me I see;
Praise Him for sufficient to eat and to wear,
While half-naked wretches go hungry and bare;
Praise Him for calm reason, that gift above all,
While, shattered and ruined, far greater minds fall.

Praise God for conviction, when worn and distressed,
That sorrows He sends me must be for the best;
Praise Him for the griefs on whose chastening wings
My soul soars to higher and holier things;
And, all through life's journey yet lying before,
Through living and dying, Praise God evermore!

North Fayette, Me., Dec. 26th, 1889.

GOD'S LETTER.

We had come from a warm, sunny country,
  Where cold, icy winds never blow,
To a land that in winter is covered
  With a mantle of feathery snow.

We had carried our wee little Lillie,
  With heaven's own light in her eyes,
Far away from her home where forever
  Smile fairest of soft summer skies.

One cold, chilling day in the autumn,
  When dark clouds hung heavy and gray,
I heard the sweet voice of my darling
  Peal out with its laughter so gay.

And I found the fair, sweet little maiden
  With snow-crystals bright in her curls,
Catching at the light flakes as they eddied
  On the breezes in airiest whirls.

And as I gazed lovingly on her,
  She caught a white snow-flake so broad,
And dimpling with mirth and with laughter
  She cried, "See my letter from God."

That night came a cough hard and ringing
  From the dear little innocent's bed,
Telling of childhood's scourge, and ere morning
  Our beautiful darling was dead !

She had flown from our shelter forever,
  Her blue eyes would never unfold,
Her sweet laughter never would cheer us,
  Or her bright, tossing ringlets of gold.

When we buried our beautiful darling
  To her rest 'neath the snow-covered sod,
We felt in the midst of our weeping
  She indeed had a message from God.

And we knew in the Land of the Blesséd
  He had opened His loving arms wide,
To receive the reply to His letter,
  Forever to rest at His side.

Long Island, Me., Jan. 11th, 1887.

LOVE LYRICS.

DRIFTED APART.

They parted under the midnight moon, while the pale stars
    throbbed on high ;
And the zephyrs sighed, and the dew-drops bright like
    tears on the grass-blades shone,
All the cherished dreams of the past destroyed, and broken
    each tender tie,
And with one consent to the life before each sadly pressed
    on alone.

They had been nearer by far than friends when the morning
    of life shone bright,
And its first fond dream, heaven-sweet to all, found place
    in each youthful heart ;
But all things had changed, they could scarce tell how, as
    the shades of a falling night
O'ercast the glorious, golden west; they only drifted
    apart.

No quarrel had on life's quiet broke, and no great wrong
    their hopes o'erthrown,
But a doubt, a shadow that grew apace, crept between them
    and would not go ;
And somehow further apart they drew, till their cherished
    plans, all outgrown,
Were cast forever from both that night, each half wishing
    things not so.

Both misunderstood, and the doubt once formed had
  shattered the golden spell,
Till all was over between two hearts that once might have
  beat as one,
And a change was made, either good or bad, whose effect
  neither then could tell;
He passed away from her side that night, and the things of
  the past were done.

Two lives, close-welded, broke sharp apart, yet tender
  remained the breach,
Though years rolled on, and the parted pair strove to
  banish memories dead.
New ties were formed and new hopes indulged, yet a
  sorrow remained to each;
And neither ever could quite forget the hours that for aye
  were fled.

The years passed by, and again they met; both were
  softened and changed at heart,
For each could see with the other's eyes, by time's
  experience taught,
And their severed lives in a moment touched where once
  they were torn apart,
And grew in one like a fresh-made wound, — but too late
  were these changes wrought.

Alas for the things that one time had been, yet never could
      be again !
Alas for the things that might have been !   And alas for
     . the things that were !
Too late they saw as they should have seen when their
      spirits were rent in twain ;
But that time was fled and the die was cast — and alas for
      both him and her !

No earthly power could straighten all for their own hearts
      had willed it so,
Though they met again and all things were clear.   Was it
      better so ?   Who can tell ?
And again they parted to meet no more, as they parted
      long years ago,
And, gazing back where their paths diverged, each sadly
      thought, ''Was it well?''

Long Island, Me., Sept. 9th, 1888.

OUR MEETING.

We shall meet on some day of the future,
  Hand to hand, heart to heart, brow to brow ;
Once again shall we greet one another,
  But, alas ! nothing will be as now.

We shall meet beyond changes we dream not,
  For things that are now will not be,
And things will then be that now are not ;
  How will it be with you and me ?

Shall we meet with fond, loving embraces,
  With hand-clasps, and kisses, and smiles ?
Or with sorrow's self-evident traces
  Of sighs and of tear-drops the whiles ?

Shall we meet as friends meet in the future,
  As dearest ones parted for long ?
Or as strangers view each well-known feature,
  Forgetting hours sweet as a song ?

Shall we meet in warm life as we parted ?
  Or in dark, funereal gloom
Will one stand all alone, broken-hearted,
  While the other is laid in the tomb ?

Shall we meet in the Land of the Shadows,
    When our pulses have finished their beat,
In a realm where earth's care never follows,
    And the tale of this life is complete?

Shall we look back in sorrow behind us
    On the wrecks and the ruins of years?
Shall we see in the hours that have passed us
    A record of folly and tears?

Or will the days, peacefully gliding,
    Flow softly from time's silver urn
In a smooth stream, too calm for vain sighing
    For moments that never return?

God alone knows when cometh the meeting,
    Where, and whether in pleasure or tears,
But some day we'll see it and, standing
    Side by side, we'll look back on the years.

We shall see our paths winding like rivers,
    Our joys, and our sorrows, and tears,
Our hopes, and our plans, and endeavors,
    Our failures, and follies, and fears.

We shall meet — but the world will be altered;
    We shall meet — but in us will be change;
We shall meet, not, alas! as we parted!
    How we know not, but all will be strange.

Long Island, Me., Feb. 3rd, 1887.

THE ACACIA TREE.

The spring is coming back amain,
  The winter soon will flee,
And vernal beauty hill and plain
  Will render fair to see,
And fragrant flowers bloom again
  On the acacia tree.

I love the scented blossoms fair
  As dearly as the bee
That revels in the sweetness there;
  And yet they bring to me
Sad dreams of vanished moments rare
  'Neath an acacia tree.

My sorrow-laden spirit grieves
  O'er the sweet memory
Of one of spring's most perfect eves,
  That nevermore will be,
When moon-rays glistened through the leaves
  Of an acacia tree.

There stood within its shadow sweet
  A maiden fair to see,
The breeze strewed blossoms at her feet,
  As her lips breathed to me
A vow too sacred to repeat,
  'Neath the acacia tree.

The memory of holy love
  The pure one felt for me
From my heart nothing can remove;
  Her last, dear gift I see
With tears, — dead blooms she plucked above
  From the acacia tree.

That eve is in the buried past,
  And her no more I see.
A shadow on my life was cast,
  That only left to me
A mound o'er which, in every blast,
  Moans an acacia tree.

North Fayette, Me., Jan. 3rd, 1890.

THE WALK UNTAKEN.

The friend of a long past spring-time,
    When the warm days had come again,
And the buds of a coming summer
    Were swelling on hill and plain,
Said to me, with a smile of patience,
    " When the summer winds kiss the brow,
We will go on a long, long ramble ;
    I am too weak and tired now."

The days of the summer hastened,
    And the landscape was bright and fair,
And the leaf and the bird-song trembled
    Afar in the sunset air ;
And I said, "Let us walk together,
    For the evening is fair and still."
But she said, " I am still aweary ;
    In the autumn I surely will."

In the days of the early autumn,
    When the harvest was ripening fast,
And the fields with their crops abundant
    Shone in beauty too bright to last,
" Let us take the long-promised ramble,"
    I said, as the warm sun set,
And again did she smile upon me,
    But sighed as she said, "Not yet."

Ere the snows of the winter drifted
  O'er the leaves of a summer dead,
The sod of the valley covered
  Forever that fair young head;
And the feet, once too weak to ramble
  With me, had outstripped my own,
And gone on a long, long journey
  To the summer land alone.

Her form was no longer weary,
  But our ramble was not to be;
And never in earthly sunshine
  Will she wander along with me.
But some day my feet will travel
  To the land where our lost ones dwell,
And we may take that walk together
  In the meadows of asphodel.

Portland, Me., Feb. 4th, 1888.

SONG.

You're far away from me, dear ;
  To fate's decree I bow ;
I know that it must be, dear,
  But, oh! I'm lonely now.

You were my soul's delight, dear ;
  Why should we have to part?
You vanished from my sight, dear,
  But never from my heart.

While you are far away, dear,
  Your influence is here ;
Though absent many a day, dear,
  To me you're ever near.

It turns me from the wrong, dear,
  Your influence within ;
'Tis gentle, but 'tis strong, dear,
  In shielding me from sin.

I'm better, that I feel, dear,
  Since first your worth I knew ;
Thoughts of you make appeal, dear,
  To all that's good and true.

You've changed me for the best, dear ;
  Thoughts of you change me still,
And without stop or rest, dear,
  They guide, and always will.

Alas ! I can not say, dear,
  If we again shall meet ;
God in love grant we may, dear,
  And speed the moment sweet !

Long Island, Me., Jan. 17th, 1887.

I DREAMED THAT I WAS DEAD.

I dreamed that I was dead,
And in my last, long rest was laid away
Under the ground, far from the light of day;
Above my head the summer breezes blew,
The buds and blossoms reared their heads anew,
The sunshine glanced, the brooklet murmured by,
The glad birds sang, delighting ear and eye
Of living ones; all these were round me spread;
      And I was dead!

I dreamed that I was dead,
And o'er my brow a gentle footstep came;
I heard dear, well-known lips repeat my name;
I felt warm tears fall on the grass-grown sod
That sundered our two faces; ah, dear God!
The bitter lot, to lie, and feel, and know
My love wept close to me in sorest woe!
I could not soothe; the grave-mould hid my head;
      For I was dead!

I dreamed that I was dead,
And yet the thought of a life incomplete
Tortured my heart, though it had ceased to beat ;
The thought of moments wasted, thrown away,
Of opportunities then lost for aye,
Of good deeds that I might and should have wrought,
Of wrongs I might have righted, and did not,
Of bays that one day might have crowned my head,
        But I was dead !

I dreamed that I was dead,
But yet, thank God ! it was a dream alone,
And time and chance for much are yet my own.
Please Him that when this earthly body dies,
The sod forever hides my sightless eyes,
If thought or feeling yet should be my own,
I may not mourn thus o'er the moments flown
That left so little good behind me spread,
        When I am dead !

Long Island, Me., May 15th, 1888.

PARTED.

Yes! for aye the tie is broken, and the die is ever cast,
The bright dream forever shattered; far too bright, alas!
       to last;
We can ne'er be to each other as we have been in the past.

Our lives must divide forever, like our paths which lead
       apart;
Pluck the past from out the memory, the loved image from
       the heart;
Let us turn unto the future and forget the hidden smart.

You were not what I believed you; the scales fell, and I
       could see;
Nor was I what you had thought me, naught alike in you
       and me;
But 'tis over! Oh how sad 'tis such mistakes should ever
       be!

We have parted; to the future we have sadly turned our
       feet,
And the dead past lies behind us, full of sadness, yet how
       sweet!
God knows if in life's arena we again may chance to meet.

It perchance may happen some day that our lives may
    cross again,
Ere for us Time's ceaseless currents reach Eternity's wide
    main ;
Should it happen, will the meeting bring to us no shade of
    pain ?

If it chance that in the future face to face again we stand,
But as strangers, and as strangers part with just a clasp of
    hand,
Will there not arise before us that mistake, the severed
    band ?

Though the past be dead forever, and we ne'er can be the
    same
As we have been, the old errors will burn like a hidden
    flame ;
Yet not we, the Power that made us as we were, must bear
    the blame.

Though in time all our mistakings we may view without
    regret,
Still we ne'er can meet each other as though we had never
    met ;
Though we may appear as strangers, yet we never can
    forget.

Port Republic, N. J., Feb. 4th, 1886.

TO ELLIE.

Ellie, my darling, you know not how near to me
　The years have bound you, my love and my life;
Absence but makes you more needful and dear to me;
　God speed the moment that makes you my wife!

Oh, what a glory the bright years have borne to me,
　Since the fond moment that made you my own!
Keep the sweet vow that your pure lips have sworn to me,
　And poor to me were a king on his throne.

Waking or sleeping, I think of you, dream of you,
　Ellie, my love, and my life, and my all!
Fair is the world when my eyes catch a gleam of you,
　But is a desert when vainly I call.

Absent or present, 'tis you I am sighing for,
　The one great blessing I beg and implore.
You, only you, love, my spirit is crying for;
　Come to me, Ellie, and leave me no more.

Come to me, darling, and soothe me and sing to me,
　Light of my life and the hope of my heart,
Come to me, darling, and kiss me and cling to me,
　While life is ours nevermore to depart.

Beautiful one, be yourself and be true to me ;
  And to doubt you were to doubt the divine,
And I care not what false fortune may do to me
  If you, sweet Ellie, forever are mine;

Mine evermore, for your pure lips express it so
  In a soft whisper just over your breath ;
What is my life, dear, that your love should bless it so,
  Ellie, mine only, in life and in death ?

North Fayette, Me., Dec. 29th, 1889.

LONGINGS.

I sigh for the sight of a wild-rose face,
    And faint for the touch of a fair white hand,
As I dream of a figure of lightsome grace,
    With a yearning lovers can understand.
I long for a look from the love-lit eyes
That can not conceal what within them lies,
For the lips whose sweetness I learned to prize,
    And I see but the empty space.

For the face like a primrose, to me so dear,
    Has fled forever from out my way,
And the tender touch of a vanished year
    And the fairy figure are gone for aye.
I shall only see in the world above
Those starry eyes with their looks of love,
But the ripe lips' sweetness I there may prove,
    That on earth nevermore I may.

Though my aching heart in the darkness call,
　　It is all in vain, for no answers come;
And darker and deeper the shadows fall,
　　For the lips I list for on earth are dumb.
Nevermore will my own cling quivering there;
My arms are empty, my life is bare;
What years are bringing I scarcely care,
　　For my future is wrapped in gloom.

North Fayette, Me., Dec. 25th, 1889.

UNDER THE STARS.

Have you forgotten our first evening ramble,
  Down in the lane where the whip-poor-will sang,
Hid in the hedgerow of brier and bramble,
  Where the old apple-trees over it hang?
  Don't you remember that walk to the gate,
      Under the stars?

Your modest features drooped under my gazing,
  And strange, new feelings my young bosom stirred;
My bashful arm round you daringly raising,
  (I saw you blush, but you said not a word!)
  I drew your slight figure close to my side,
      Under the stars. .

I felt your heart's wild, tumultuous leaping,
  As to my bosom I gathered your form;
When your shy eyes to mine slowly came creeping —
  How could I help it? — your dewy lips warm
  My own just touched in a scared, hurried kiss,
      Under the stars.

Ah ! we were young, and a fairy-like splendor
 Lightened our lives then that now we have lost,
And love's first beauty, bewitching and tender,
 Dawned for us both as the dim lane we crossed,
 Strange and so sweet we knew not what it was;
  Under the stars.

But we have parted, and parted forever;
 That love matured not as years hurried by ;
Often I dreamily wonder if ever
 You think of that night as fondly as I,
 And sigh as memory pictures the walk
  Under the stars.

North Fayette, Me., Jan. 2nd, 1890.

MIZPAH.

Friend of my youth, we have parted in sorrow;
  Our paths divided long winters ago,
Never to cross but in Heaven's to-morrow,
  When we have finished our journey below.
        Mountain and river,
        And forests that quiver,
  Part from the face that no longer I see ;
        Tenderly sighing
        As moments are flying,
  I pray, "The Lord watch between thee and me!"

Sweet were those hours when we wandered together,
  Weaving the bright, golden fancies of youth,
But life is changing as midsummer weather ;
  Fairest ideals gave place to the truth.
        Visions have faded,
        And sorrows invaded ;
  Closely linked hearts have been parted for years ;
        Hopes that were cherished
        So fondly have perished,
  Leaving a record of folly and tears.

. Loved one and lost one, no more I behold you,
    Yet still affection is warm in my soul;
Though so long absent, my heart-strings enfold you
    But the more closely as years onward roll.
        Brightness surround you,
        'Till seraphs have crowned you!
Peace be your own till time ceases to be!
        All joys be given
        Until you gain Heaven,
And " May the Lord watch between thee and me!''

North Fayette, Me., Dec. 31st, 1889.

STELLA.

I think of you to-night, love,
  As evening shadows fall ;
The shining orbs of light, love,
  Your starry eyes recall.
Through all the years I've known you,
Star of my soul I own you,
And in my heart enthrone you, .
  My only and my all !

To me you're ever near, love,
  Though waste and waters part ;
Your wild-rose face is here, love,
  Close hidden in my heart.
In memory or dreaming,
Your star-eyes, brightly gleaming,
Are always on me beaming ;
  They nevermore depart.

If God's love think it right, dear,
  Our lives should part for aye,
My earthly star in night, dear,
  Set on my darkened way,
As death divides forever
The hearts that ache to sever,
My memory will ever
  Retain its parting ray.

And faith will bridge the wave, dear,
    The torrent's streaming bar
Poured from an open grave, dear,
    That hides the world afar;
And when I sadly ponder,
As lone and lorn I wander,
I'll feel that over yonder
    I'll hail my Morning Star.

North Fayette, Me., Dec. 31st, 1889.

O, DEEP, DARK EYES!

O, deep, dark, melting, beautiful eyes,
  As fathomless, clear, as the deep, dark sea,
Tell to me the secret that in you lies,
  The wealth of your wonderful mystery!
The hidden feelings that ebb and flow,
The thoughts unuttered that come and go,
The things I know not, but fain would know,
  O, dear eyes, reveal to me!

O, eyes that timidly gaze on mine,
  And then turn in coyness or modesty,
Interpret the thoughts that within you shine;
  Their hidden meaning make known to me!
I can not fathom your depths aright,
The changing gleam in your shadowy light;
I would fain believe, if I only might,
  What sometimes I think I see.

O, Deep, Dark Eyes !

O, deep, dark eyes, with your glances fond,
  O, eyes so tender, and pure, and true,
Through you let me gaze to the soul beyond,
  And read there the story that's ever new !
Disclose the secret you guard so well ;
Confirm or shatter the golden spell,
What the lips speak not, let your glances tell ;
  Do you love me as I love you ?

Long Island, Me., April 30th, 1888.

THE DIFFERENCE.

They plighted truth in the days of youth,
  With a kiss and a clasp of hand,
But with thoughts of each, underlying speech,
  As unlike as the sea and sand.

He gave in part his aspiring heart,
  But his ambitious schemes were more
Than the jewel rare he had but to wear,
  More precious than crown ere bore.

She brought the whole of a spotless soul;
  Her life and her love, her all,
To fling at his feet in an offering sweet
  She might never again recall.

Tender dreams of her would his spirit stir,
  When his toil, for the time, was done,
But ere long the strife and the cares of life
  Banished thoughts of the waiting one.

But she dreamed of him, as her eyes grew dim,
  At morning, at noon, at night ;
And naught could tear from the maiden fair
  The image she thought so bright.

In the inmost goal of her snow-white soul
  She had throned him, a king, a god,
At whose shrine apart, on his sordid heart,
  She could lavish love's holy flood.

But a golden wand in Fame's beckoning hand
  Soon summoned, and he obeyed ;
And, following on from the true heart won,
  Scarcely missed the deserted maid.

While she, ah ! she saw her idol flee,
  And the springs of her life stood still ; *
And its light went out in the shades of doubt
  That her love vainly strove to kill.

In a distant clime, at an idle time,
  " Just to keep the little girl still,"
He a few lines penned, dreaming not the end,
  Caring only his part to fill.

But they met too late the fond eyes in wait ;
  They were earth-dim, and faint her breath ;
And she vainly strove in her mighty love
  To read what she clasped in death.

And the foolish note that her idol wrote,
  Thoughtless, careless of what he said,
Is unread to-day, buried far away
  In the hand of the holy dead.

Long Island, Me., Nov. 21st, 1889.

MISCELLANEOUS POEMS.

THE MANIAC.

I.

Oh, the hard and pitiless doom
Of pacing around one narrow room,
Whether without is the winter's gloom,
Or summer time with its bird and bloom !
Better, far better, the silent tomb,
    If one did not fear to die !

Walking on in a narrow round,
Hemmed by four walls' merciless bound,
Alone in a solitude, dead, profound,
The maniac yelling the only sound,
And nowhere a covering to be found
    From God's all-seeing eye !

Tongue can never the terrors tell
Of a living death in a narrow cell,
Haunted by visions dark and fell,
While passions fierce in the bosom swell,
Worse than those of the damned in hell,
    For punishment of the bad.

The same small circle to pace again,
Under a curse like the curse of Cain,
My hands still red with a gory stain,
And suffering pangs of remorseful pain,
With a demon stamping upon my brain, —
    Who says that I am mad?

II.

O, Liberty !   Sweet are thy peaceful ways,
    Sweet to wander abroad at will,
And spend as pleases the joyful days,
In the quiet home or the forest maze !
With others, or far from all human gaze,
    Thine hours will be pleasant still !

Sweet Freedom's banner, oft stained with blood,
    Is dear to the patriot's eyes,
And it rises purer though dragged in mud,
For heroes' veins pour a cleansing flood,
As they bleed for the stars its folds bestud ;
    And Freedom's light never dies.

Her spirit floats in the sunset air,
    Under every sky and clime.
She lives where Oppression spreads his snare,
She is nursed by martyred patriots' prayer,
She breathes in nature everywhere,
    'Mid slavery, vice and crime.

To tame the partridge men try in vain;
  It dies in captivity.
The winds of heaven scorn curb and rein,
And of old the Hellespont's restless main
Flung off in derision the Persian's chain;
  Nature's children should all be free.

It has been the same since the days of yore,
  The pages of history tell.
'Tis Israel's record in sacred lore,
'Tis witnessed by Scotland's fields of gore,
By crimson plains on America's shore;
  All pulses for freedom swell.

If moral bondage bring such a fear
  To those God created free,
What can the lot of the lost one cheer,
Forever robbed of the sunlight clear,
Imprisoned ever by cold walls drear,
  In a hell like this made for me?

III.

No wonder I think of my childhood,
  Of the beautiful long ago,
When I wandered through field and wildwood,
  With never a thought of woe;
That I think of the ones who loved me
  In the days of the golden yore,
Now gone to the realms above me,
  And lost to me evermore;

That I think of the proud ambitions
　　Of a happy and far-off time,
That met with such curst fruitions
　　When my spirit was stained with crime;
That I think of my school-day honors,
　　When Wisdom unrolled her scroll,
Ere the temptings that fall upon us
　　Had blackened my sinless soul!

And I feel like a ruined angel,
　　When I dwell on that innocence,
Ere I saw fierce passion change all
.　Into blackness deep and dense;
Ere the wreck of my soul immortal
　　Wrought its bitterness and pain;
Ere for life closed my iron portal;
　　Ere a fiend trampled on my brain.

I long for those days, with yearning
　　That never can be expressed,
When I felt love's pure flame burning,
　　On the altar within my breast;
When I felt my strong will swaying
　　At the touch of a lovely girl,
'Twixt hope and despair delaying,
　　Fast bound by a silken curl.

IV.

Her form was as slight as a fairy,
   Full, rounded and soft ;
Her motions as graceful and airy
   As leaves up aloft.

Her eyes were as blue as the heaven
   In the dazzling June ;
Her voice seemed like sweet echoes given
   By angelic tune.

Her teeth were like pearls of the ocean
   In pink-tinted shell ;
Her red lips, at rest or in motion,
   Of bliss seemed to tell.

Her throat was of pure, spotless whiteness,
   Like marble or snow ;
Her curls with a rich, golden brightness
   In sunlight would glow.

Ah me, that such wonderful beauty
   Should be but a curse
To drag me from pleasure and duty
   To black hell — or worse !

The day the sweet promise was given,
   That she would be mine,
I seemed not on earth, but in heaven,
   In rapture divine !

V.

In a dream I went home to my cottage, while rainbows
seemed round me to play,
And all of the blessings I sighed for seemed showering
down on my way.
Of joy far too deep I was drinking, too bright were my
visions to last.
Ye gods! how it tortures the present to think of the bliss
of the past!

Around me the sweet birds were singing, their songs bore
the burden of love;
The flowers about me were springing, the sunlight poured
down from above;
The future was radiant before me, my life was unspotted
by sin;
Friends many, head filled with earth's wisdom, and never
a demon within!

I pass to the dreadful unveiling, when all things I rightfully
saw,
When the demon passed into my being, and his devilish
will became law,
When I started to visit my darling on a glorious evening
in June,
And swift through the woodland I hurried, half lit by the
light of the moon.

VI.

Great God ! what did I see
Under a spreading tree,
    Myself unseen ?
The girl I loved the best
Pressed to a rival's breast
    'Neath branches green !

Loved, did I say before ?
Worshipped, adored !   Far more
    Was she to me
Than life, or light, or love
Of man or God above !
    My all was she !

I felt a deadly blow
When, with voice soft and low,
    Her love she told.
Then, when I knew her false,
I felt each bounding pulse
    Grow still and cold.

I saw him kiss her there,
In the dim, dusky air,
    Beneath the tree.
Great God, that rulest men,
Why didst not there and then
    Slay them — or me?

VII.

Over me amid the larches,
Black among the leafy arches,
   Leaned a tree,
Seared and lifeless, hollow, riven,
Blackened by the bolts of heaven,
When God played his thunder-marches'
   Symphony.

Cursed by Him, the fire descended
From on high, with anger blended,
   Scathed and slew ;
Cursed by man, for one fair dawning,
There the early rays of morning
Found a suicide suspended,
   Cold and blue.

In its curst and blackened hollow,
Like a huge mouth gaped to swallow
   Beast and fowl,
Dwelt a greedy, gaunt, ungainly,
Ghostly, ghastly bird, that plainly
Needless slaughter loved to follow,
   A great owl.

Nightly, while the ruin lasted,
From that old tree, thunder-blasted,
   Dark and dead,
Round about the bird went flying,
Slaying, feasting on the dying,
Till the dawn, then homeward hasted,
   Talons red.

Such the story as men know it;
All who dwelt near by could show it,
   That old tree !
But they had a darker history,
Bird and tree; a blacker mystery
That was, as I stood below it,
   Shown to me.

That tree was a thing of evil,
A place for unhallowed revel
   Fit for hell.
In its hollow there were lurking
Fiends from Hades, black charms working,
And the bird contained a devil
   Fierce and fell.

As I stood there, peering, stooping,
Loud there came a hooting, whooping,
  Sudden, dread,
And the horrid bird descended
On my brow, by naught defended ;
The fiend left the bird, while swooping,
  For my head.

In my brain he made his dwelling,
And his curséd will impelling
  Spurred me on.
When they left, this fiend, my master,
Drove me after, and disaster
Almost beyond mortal telling
  Came ere morn.

VIII.

Oh, why did she stand at the gate
  Alone, when my rival was gone?
  The fiend was impelling me on ;
Why lingered she, for it was late?

Why did the fiend torture me,
  In the pain that her falseness cost,
  With the sight of the beauty lost,
That the white moon let me see?

Why did my senses whirl
With a madness I can not tell,
With pangs like the pangs of hell,
At the sight of a faithless girl?

Why did the fiend bid rise
The sprites of Revenge and Pain,
Never to be expelled again,
While she was before my eyes?

IX.

" Crush !   Crush !"
Said the fiend within my head.
"Stretch her at your feet, dead !
Crush ! crush !

"Slay !   Slay !
With no pitying glance behind,
She slaughtered your peace of mind !
Slay ! slay !

" Kill !   Kill
The fair and the pitiless flirt,
Who gave you your mortal hurt !
Kill ! kill !

" Smite !   Smite
The source whence your curses fell,
The tortures of damned in hell !
Smite ! smite !"

X.

A single spring to the false one's side,
　　A single clutch at the fair white neck,
A clutch that lasted until she died
　　And the tide of life met an awful check !

The brilliant curls, in a tangle tossed
　　No longer glistened like burnished gold ;
Their smoothness and beauty forever lost ;
　　A snarl on a brow that would soon be cold.

The lovely skin of a snowy white,
　　That made men toys in her dainty hands,
Turned black with grim Death's horrible blight
　　As my fingers tightened their strangling bands.

The blue lips, parted in ghastly grin,
　　Displayed the teeth of a gleaming white ;
The tongue, hanging out o'er the dimpled chin,
　　Showed swollen, purple, by pale moon's light.

The lovely eyes of celestial blue,
　　Protruded in terror and deep despair,
Displaced, distended, of awful hue,
　　Were fixed on mine in a fiendish stare.

Then the limp head dropped on the tender breast
　　Life's current in those veins no more would run.
The still form sank in the dust to rest,
　　And the demon's devilish work was done.

The form that but one short hour ago
 Was clothed in beauty bright as the day,
Instinct with life, with no thought of woe,
 In the dirt a horrible ruin lay.

Oh, that homeward course through the awful night,
 Spurred on by the visions of guilty fear!
The fiend on my brain stamped in hellish might,
 With legions of devils hovering near!

They shrieked and yelled o'er my ruined soul
 In tones I shall hear till my dying day,
And I saw their fiery eyeballs roll,
 As they swooped to clutch and bear me away.

To the home of childhood I wildly fled ;
 None saw me in through the portal creep ;
And, tortured and maddened, I went to bed,
 But not to sleep — ah ! not to sleep ! ·

XI.

Dragged on the morn,
At the early dawn,
To a dungeon dark and bare,
While a mob outside
In its fury cried
For my limbs into shreds to tear !

Left all alone
In its walls of stone
To think of what I had done,
Wild with the pain
Of a bursting brain
That the demon still stamped upon !

Burn the rack and wheel,
And the boots of steel,
For tortures ye ne'er can find
That can e'er compare
With one's black despair
Alone with his guilty mind !

Words can never tell
What that awful cell,
Where I in the dim light lay,
Of suffering knew,
While I tortured through
The hours till the second day.

Stretched on iron bed,
With a bursting head,
Worn out with my ravings wild,
In a heap I lay
The following day,
As weak as a little child.

Soon I heard the swell
Of a funeral bell,
From the church tower across the way,
And its iron tongue,
As it slowly swung,
Told my victim's burial day.

XII.

Tolling, tolling,
Through the grated window rolling
Came the pealing of the bell,
Ringing Beauty's solemn knell,
To her slayer unconsoling ;
Tolling, tolling !

Pealing, pealing,
Solemn echoes round me stealing
Told of youth laid in the tomb,
'Mid corruption, worms and gloom,
Spoiled of beauty, sense and feeling ;
Pealing, Pealing !

Sobbing, sobbing,
Sad, funereal music throbbing,
Wave of sound succeeding wave
Over murdered beauty's grave ;
Death a gem of life was robbing ;
Throbbing, sobbing !

Knelling, knelling,
The last solemn service telling
Over dead clay laid away,
Till God's awful judgment day;
'Soon the last bell-notes came swelling;
Knelling, knelling!

XIII.

Silence sudden, awful, deep;
And they left her there to sleep,
As night's shades began to creep.

She was cut down in her bloom;
Hurried by a dreadful doom,
Unprepared, into the tomb.

She was thrust among the dead,
With her sins upon her head,
Ere her nineteenth year had fled.

But her fate far better is,
And less dismal far, than his
Who slew her, with its miseries.

At the midnight hour I strode
Where the grated window showed
Church and yard across the road.

In the city of the dead,
There I saw a lowly bed,
With no stone to mark its head.

There the moonlight shone above
White-winged shapes, each like a dove,
Floating o'er my murdered love.

Angels o'er the low mound hung,
On it pearly droplets flung,
While this requiem was sung:

XIV.

" Scatter the drops of forgetfulness
　　Over the false and fair ;
Let her sins sleep till the judgment day
Where in the earth she is laid away,
　　And breathe for her soul a prayer.

" Scatter the drops of forgetfulness
　　Over the sin she knew ;
Let her wrong-doing forever sleep
Here in the grave where she's buried deep ;
　　Think of her deeds good and true.

" Scatter the drops from the Lethean wave
　　Over her actions wrong ;
Think of the good she has scattered abroad,
Leaving the rest to a pitying God ;
　　His mercy endureth long !

"Scatter forgiveness above her grave;
  Leave her to a dreamless sleep!
Over the spot where her form is laid,
Let all hard feelings forever fade
  And sink in oblivion deep!"

xv.

A softness entered my weary breast
With the strain, and the demon gave me rest.
I sought the bed and a peaceful sleep
Buried my soul in a torpor deep.

They brought me out at an early day;
To this mad-house then I was borne away;
And here I suffer from year to year,
With nothing but insane shrieks to-hear.

How long I have been here I cannot tell,
In a living grave, in an earthly hell!
I am not mad, as all men aver,
I am not!   I almost wish I were!

Oh, if I could but the past forget!
If I could but die in my sleep — and yet,
My ruined soul is the Devil's own;
He only waits till my life is done.

I am not, I tell you, I am not mad!
I wonder I am not, I am so bad;
And, with a fiend pounding my aching brain,
It is strange to me I am not insane.

He is walking now in my throbbing head ;
My skull resounds with his heavy tread.
O, God in heaven !   Thy lost one bless,
By blotting him out into nothingness !

XVI.

He is stamping now
  With a red-hot hoof;
He dances and yells
  'Neath my skull's arched roof.

The quivering brain
  In my throbbing brow
With his fiery nails
  He is tearing now.

He gnaws its fibers
  With venomed jaws ;
He plucks my eyeballs
  With blazing claws.

Great God, have mercy !
  Oh, strike me dead !
Satan, call thy servant
  From out my head !

Oh, hell and torment !
  I'll dash you out
On the pitiless stone walls
  Round about !

] will tear you out
  With my furious hands !
But no — the firm bone
  My strength withstands !

'Tis useless !   The Lord
  And the Devil as well
Have doomed me, living,
  To worse than hell !

Vain, vain, though the cell walls
  Around are red
With hair, blood-clotted,
  Dashed from my head !

XVII.

But hark ! a murmur runs along the wall,
And blue flame-flashes flicker, fade and fall,
  Now — blackness all !

Again they come ; they brighten, blue and cold,
All but one corner that the shadows hold.
  See ! they unfold !

See ! see ! my murdered love ; see ! there she stands,
Just as I saw her dying in my hands ;
  Vengeance demands !

Her face all black with choking still appears,
But mildewed with the grave-mould of long years ;
  At me she leers !

Her eyes are forced out of their proper place
Half finger length ; they glare across the space
   Into my face !

The long, black tongue, the horrid, fallen jaw,
Have withered, blackened in the charnel's maw ;
   Sight full of awe !

Open, ye solid walls, and swallow me
From sight too fearful for a man to see
   And yet to be !

God ! Satan ! Heaven ! Hell ! one ! any ! all !
Oh, save me from that specter by the wall
   In shroud and pall !

She comes ! Help ! help ! Oh, spare me, spare me, thou !
Pity, forgiveness for my crime allow !
   Oh spare me now !

Long years of torture, grief, remorse, regret,
Have been my lot and portion since we met.
   Oh, spare me yet !

I long repented what I did to thee.
'Twas not I, but the fiend that entered me,
   Set your soul free !

What, gone ? And has she left me ? Yes ; 'tis so !
I tremble ! Icy breezes on me blow !
   Cold sweat-drops flow !

My eyes are burning in my aching brow ;
The awful specter's fled, I know not how,
   That late — What now !

XVIII.

Back, you awful apparition,
  ' With your red eyes flashing fire,
With your every breath's emission
   Belching sulphur-vapors dire !
Each hideous feature on your face
Warped up and twisted out of place !

Go, you gaunt and grisly goblin,
   Wrinkled-skinned and bacon-hued,
On your red-hot, split hoofs hobbling,
   With your claws with blood imbrued,
With your live, hissing, snaky hair,
Spitting black venom everywhere !

Yes, old Satan ! Well I know you,
   With your dark form dripping fire,
With your forky tail below you
   Smeared in hell's black poison-mire,
Away ! I will not go with you
To the hot realm from which you flew !

XIX.

   Great God ! Let go,
   You fiend of woe !
Your red-hot talons pierce me through !
The dripping hell-fire falls on me and sticks to me like
   glue.

The serpents dread
That crown your head
Gnaw deep into my quivering flesh,
Spitting their cankering venom as they tear each wound
afresh !

The sickening fume
Pervades the room !
You tear me with your fiendish claws
To fragments ! Oh, I never knew what hellish torment
was !

My quick flesh fries
Before your eyes !
The poison from your features grim
Cankers and festers, eating vein and sinew from each
limb.

O, Heaven on high
Hear my good-bye !
Who says I'm mad? What stops my breath?
Ha, ha ! I am a devil now ! Great God, can this be
death ?

Long Island, Me., Dec. 30-31, 1884.

A RUIN.

Lone, deserted, stands the dwelling
   That was home long years ago,
And the mildewed rooms are vacant
   That have echoed joy and woe;
Sagging beam and doorless portal,
   Crumbling wall and shattered floor,
Plainly tell their mournful story
   Of the feet that come no more.

Broken is the roof dismantled,
   And the storms of heaven pour
Through its holes and rotten rafters
   On the moldy attic floor.
Only bat, and bird, and beetle
   In the empty chambers hide,
Where men slept and where they suffered,
   Where they lived and where they died.

Fallen chimneys, broken hearthstones,
   In the cellar blended lie,
Whose bright, merry blaze up-flashing
   Warmed and cheered in days gone by;
But no more the back-log's sparkle
   Lights the dim, decaying room,
Once a glad home's happy refuge,
   Now sad, silent as a tomb!

Brier-grown the pathways leading .
   To those door-stones dank with moss,
O'er whose black and broken thresholds
   Human footsteps never cross;
And the unglazed, sashless windows,
   In dull questioning surprise,
Stare away into the future
   With their vacant, spectral eyes.

They are gone, and gone forever,
   Those walls knew in days of yore;
Each and all long since departed
   To come back again no more.
Now the sad and sinking ruin,
   Blackened by the breath of years,
Tells alone they once existed
   In a world of smiles and tears.

Gone the maid, and gone the matron,
   Grandsire grey and blooming bride;
Gone the child, and gone the parent,
   Crossed beyond the swelling tide.
All forgot their pains and pleasures,
   All their plans, and prayers, and strife;
These walls are, in ruin falling,
   The sole record of their life.

May be shades of those departed
    Enter where they enter not;
May be viewless spirits hover
    Round this desolated spot.
Certainly the place is haunted
    By the thoughts and dreams of yore,
But those whom it loved and sheltered
    In the flesh return no more.

Long Island, Me., Nov. 28th, 1889.

IN THE CHURCHYARD.

Under the daisies together are lying,
  Side by side sleeping, the poor and the proud.
Rich man and pauper, alike, upon dying,
  Rest from their labor in coffin and shroud.

Little care they whether silver-plate burnished
  And costly linen lie white on the breast,
Or the rough pine wood, by charity furnished,
  And the coarse cotton protect their last rest.

Proud marble shafts of a pure, snowy whiteness
  Stand looking down on slate tombstones so small,
While close behind where they rise in their brightness,
  Green mounds are seen with no tablets at all.

Here lies the poet who once moved the nation,
  Weaving pure thoughts in his musical rhyme,
Blessing the world in the airy creation
  Of his bright fancy and genius sublime.

But the great brain in which genius was burning
  Molders to dust in this green, silent bed;
Hands of the poet to ashes are turning,
  While the blue violets wave o'er his head.

Here lies the miser, whose god was his money;
  Waiving all questions of right and of wrong,
Cruelly robbing life's flower of its honey,
  He preyed on weak ones because he was strong.

But the hard heart has forgotten its grasping;
  Hoards that he worshipped are squandered and gone;
Earth his stern form to her bosom is clasping;
  Want's grim oppressor sleeps silently on.

In this green nook a great statesman is lying,
  Whose burning eloquence swayed the whole world;
Whose glowing speeches of wisdom undying,
  On wings of lightning to distant lands whirled.

But the full voice of the statesman is silent,
  And the great mind has departed for aye,
And the grand face, with the fire that the eye lent,
  In the dark coffin has dropped to decay.   .

Here close beside him a pauper is sleeping,
  Scorned in his lifetime, despised at his death;
Living — a beggar through almshouses creeping,
  Dead — just as good as a king without breath.

Back into dust in the same field are turning
  Author and idiot, teacher and fool.
Each of them spent a whole lifetime in earning
  Six feet of earth in the old churchyard cool.

Young and old, falling before the grim reaper,
  Silently in their last home have been laid.
Tumult or care never troubles the sleeper
  Lying at rest in this green, leafy shade.

Grand aspiration and lofty emotion,
  Basest desire and groveling fear,
Feverish toil and untiring devotion,
  Ended at last, find a resting-place here.

Youthful and beautiful mortals have perished,
  Ugly and old ones have dropped to decay.
Here lies the beauty that artists have cherished;
  Here plainest features to worms fall a prey.

Under the roof of the blue dome of heaven,
  Sheltered from storms by the grasses that wave,
Here where their forms to the earth have been given, ·
  Let them rest on in embrace of the grave.

Sleeping the sleep that shall know no awaking,
  Here let them lie in their slumber profound
Till the morn of resurrection is breaking
  And the whole earth to the trump shall resound.

North Fayette, Me., Feb. 16th, 1883.

COME, SING TO ME.

Come, sing to me in the gloaming,
  As the twilight shadows fall,
And the firelight's fitful flashes
  Are flickering on the wall;
For my heart with care is burdened,
  And sad is my soul to-night,
But your voice has power to soothe me
  And make all my troubles light.

Sing not from the classic authors
  The melodies strange and wild.
But the old and the plaintive ballads
  I listened to when a child;
And then, on the wings of music
  And the sweet and tender rhyme,
My soul will go floating backward
  To the happy and olden time.

With "Sweet Home's" musical cadence
  My memory swiftly flies
To the blissful days of childhood
  And youth's fair morning skies,
And the bright days unforgotten
  In the old house on the hill;
And again as a child I wander,
  No guide but my own sweet will.

And the strains of the "Swanee River,"
  As softly around they float,
A rare blessing seem to bring me
  With every liquid note;
A pleasure that's mixed with sadness,
  For "everywhere I roam,"
That song always brings a longing
  For the dear "old folks at home."

Come sing the "Last Rose of Summer,"
  With its sweet and plaintive air,   .
For it seems to float around me
  Like the sound of an angel's prayer;
And thoughts of the ones who sang it
  In the happy days gone by
Bring the spirit a tender sadness,
  And misty light to the eye.

Such melodies bring me fancies
  And dreams of the olden times,
When I listened to other voices
  Soft breathing those dear old rhymes;
But those singers are widely scattered,
  The friendship of some grown cold;
Some distant, and some are sleeping
  Low under the churchyard mold.

Yet the old familiar ballads
 All bring me a sense of rest,
And the thoughts they cause are soothing
 To my weary and troubled breast;
And I love the dear old pieces
 I listened to years ago;
At their notes Time's resistless river
 Seems to stop in its ceaseless flow.

Then sing to me in the twilight
 Some melody old and sweet,
While the shadows of night are falling
 And the darkness becomes complete.
My mind shall go drifting backward
 To the hours of the happy past,
And peace shall replace my troubles
 While shadows are gathering fast.

North Fayette, Me., Nov. 14th, 1884.

IN DREAMLAND.

Oft, when alone, from the Land of the Shadows
  In the dead past comes my childhood to me ;
Oft in my fancy I roam o'er the meadows
  And through the forests, by mountain and lea.
But, all too soon, the bright visions departing
  Over my spirit a sadness will cast,
As, from these day-dreams of pleasure upstarting,
  I see the present and not the fair past.

Oft, in my musings, I raise the soft curtain
  Ever concealing the future from view,
And in a dreamland so sweet and uncertain
  Wander 'mid pleasures too sweet to be true.
But those light castles that fancy is rearing,
  Vanishing, leave the stern present again,
And their fair, rosy hues on disappearing
  Leave a sad feeling that's kindred to pain.

Round the past hours hangs a halo of glory,
  Rainbows of splendor to memory cling,·
Time makes them tell so enchanting a story,
  The present fair seems a pleasureless thing ;
While, in the future, a fairy-like brightness
  Beckons us on with its mystery rare ;
Striving for shadows we think not of duty,
  Or present scenes though they too may be fair.

Thus in a dreamland we mortals are living,
　　Half in the future and half in the past ;
Noting not pleasures the present is giving ;
　　Clasping the shadow while substance flies fast ;
Chasing the future that's flitting before us ;
　　Yearning o'er happy hours vanished for aye ;
Never once seeing bright skies bending o'er us,
　　Or the rich gifts of a joyous to-day.

Oh, could we value our joys ere we lose them,
　　Pick up the gems lying close at our feet,
See all our chances ere too late to use them,
　　Then would this life of ours be doubly sweet !
Distance to past and to future is lending
　　Beauties unnoticed if now they were ours ;
Briers that tear us when round they are bending
　　Before or behind us seem nothing but flowers.

Monmouth, Me., March 25th, 1884.

GOOD-BYE.

There's a word that oft comes from the depths of the heart,
A word that oft causes the tear-drops to start,
And the quivering lip and the dim, misty eye
Tell the sorrow repressed when is breathed with a sigh
    The one word, "Good-bye!"

Good-bye! God be with you! A prayer and farewell!
How much of deep feeling two syllables tell!
Though oft lightly said when the lashes are dry,
How much still unspoken that word may imply,
    The tender good-bye!

And when it is breathed as the friend parts from friend,
Knowing not if on earth separation may end,
Feeling hearts may grow still that are now beating high,
And under the daisies forever may lie,
    How sad the good-bye!

How hard it is torn from the innermost heart
Of those who well know they forever must part!
With what grief comes then the farewell and reply!
What sorrow is breathed in the loving good-bye,
    The last, long good-bye!

And when at the bedside where life's labors close,
Where friends sink forever to death's long repose,
No wonder that tears are o'erflowing the eye,
And voice is half choked with the heart-broken sigh
     At saying good-bye!

The time is fast coming when all upon earth
Must pass on, though little or great be their worth;
The hour of departure is fast drawing nigh
When all must bid earth, with a death-closing eye,
     An eternal good-bye.

Yet tender, though sad, are the fancies that cling
Round the word that earth's partings to weeping ones bring,
And sweet, though regretful, the last, loving sigh,
The prayer, the farewell, the old, tender good-bye;
     God be with you!   Good-bye!

North Fayette, Me., Aug. 18th, 1885.

IN THE FIRELIGHT.

Softly now the evening twilight
  On the silent landscape falls,
And the great old-fashioned fireplace
  Throws its flashes on the walls.
As the flames go leaping upward
  In the chimney dark and wide,
Lights and shadows quickly changing
  Dance around on every side.

As the firelight leaps and flickers,
  And its warmth steals through the room,
And all things are alternating
  'Twixt its flashing and the gloom,
Thoughts come rushing fast upon me
  Sitting in the firelight bright.
Like its rays my fancy changes
  As I watch the shifting light.

And amid my quiet musings
  Thoughts of loved ones gone before
Seem to fill the changing shadows,
  With forms I shall see no more.
Lost ones, though still unforgotten,
  Seem once more to enter here,
And I listen for their spirits
  In the firelight drawing near.

Lovingly they cluster round me,
    And their presence I can feel,
And my soul holds sweet communion
    With those that around me steal.
Pleasant thoughts, like inspirations,
    From the shadows seem to come,
And my musings seem like breathings
    From the soul's eternal home.

Peaceful is the hour of evening
    In the dimly lighted room,
While the firelight's ruddy flashes
    Dart and quiver through the gloom.
My heart loses pains and sorrows,
    That have worn it through the day,
And care's wrinkles from my forehead
    Angels seem to smooth away.

When I think of those who sat here
    By this light, in days long past,
'Tis no wonder through the shadows
    Spirit forms seem crowding fast.
Many hearts that once were beating
    In its warm and ruddy glow,
Underneath the churchyard grasses
    Fell to dust long years ago.

Though the huge old-fashioned fireplace
    Sends a greeting to my heart
At all hours, and its bright flashes
    Always pleasant thoughts impart,
Yet 'tis at the hour of twilight
    That its blaze the dearest seems,
And the dancing lights and shadows
    Bring to me the sweetest dreams.

Blessings on the ancient fireplace,
    That has blazed for many a year!
May its wide mouth still continue
    With its warmth all hearts to cheer!
May the beech log's merry crackle
    Still be heard in days to come,
When the one who sings its praises
    Shall have reached the silent home!

North Fayette, Me., Nov. 16th, 1884.

L'ENVOI.

Go your way, my little volume, first fruits of an unpruned
    tree,
Growing wild beside the highway.   Little wonder 'tis to
    me
That its windfalls, small and shapeless, bitter acid-balls
    should be.

Harsh and untaught is my singing, haply better left
    undone;
False notes flutter through the music, jarring discords pain
    and stun ;
But through rude and Runic measures chords of sweetness
    sometimes run.

Far above, the mighty masters of poetic art divine
Breathe their strains of heavenly sweetness, passion thrilling
    through each line ;
Few and faint the feeble murmurs that re-echo back from
    mine.

Humble these, my heartfelt numbers, yet perhaps, a reader
just
Some pure thought-gems may discover in the worthless
wordy dust ;
Judge not harshly these weak efforts, for I sing because I
must.

May be I should not be silent, though no Muse with
heavenly fire
Touched my lips, and though my fingers sweep a rude and
tuneless lyre,
Though my feeble voice may never swell the Bards' angelic
choir.

Does the streamlet cease to murmur rippling music on its
way,
Just because the ocean's grandeur does not thunder through
its lay,
Or the river's rushing rhythm drowns its ever-chiming
play?

Do the faint stars cease to tremble with their pure and holy
light,
Lest the full moon dim their luster when she rises broad
and bright,
Flinging floods of pearly glory from her throne as queen
of night?

Does the wild bird cease to warble with the music in his
      heart,
When the trained and caged canary far excels him in the
      art?
So with me: my songs, unbidden, into being seem to start.

I must sing! but, little volume, ere your leaves forgotten
      lie,
If you soothe one troubled spirit, then your memory may
      die;
Your work will be well accomplished. May it be so;
      Child, good bye!

North Fayette, Me., Dec. 29th, 1889.

www.ingramcontent.com/pod-product-compliance
Lightning Source LLC
Chambersburg PA
CBHW030643030726
47497CB00006B/1922